WEAPON

THE COMPOSITE BOW

MIKE LOADES

Series Editor Martin Pegler

First published in Great Britain in 2016 by Osprey Publishing,
PO Box 883, Oxford, OX1 9PL, UK
1385 Broadway, 5th Floor, New York, NY 10018, USA
E-mail: info@ospreypublishing.com

Osprey Publishing, part of Bloomsbury Publishing Plc

A CIP catalogue record for this book is available from the British
Library

Print ISBN: 978 1 4728 0591 1
PDF ebook ISBN: 978 1 4728 2162 1
ePub ebook ISBN: 978 1 4728 2161 4

Index by Rob Munro
Typeset in Sabon and Univers
Originated by PDQ Media, Bungay, UK
Printed in China through World Print Ltd.

16 17 18 19 20   10 9 8 7 6 5 4 3 2 1

Osprey Publishing supports the Woodland Trust, the UK's leading
woodland conservation charity. Between 2014 and 2018 our
donations are being spent on their Centenary Woods project in
the UK.

www.ospreypublishing.com

The following abbreviations have been used in the accreditation
of photographs: KH = Kim Hawkins; ML = Mike Loades; UM =
Museum of Anthropology, University of Missouri.

Front cover images are © KH (above) and Osprey Publishing
(below).
Title page: Horse-archer shooting a short arrow with a *sipur*.
Note that the archer also carries his sword in his draw-hand,
even when shooting. The image is taken from a privately
commissioned replica, in the author's collection, of the *Nihāyat
al-su'l wa l-umniyya fi ta'līm a'mal al-furūsiyya*, a 14th-century
Mamluk manual of military arts. (ML)

Dedication

For Gordon Summers

Acknowledgements

I owe an old debt of gratitude to Edward McEwen, who first
introduced me to the enchantment of composite bows. A scholar
and a maker of fine bows, Ted was also a practising horse-archer
long before it became the phenomenon it is today. He has been
an inspiration. As the long-serving editor of the *Journal of the
Society of Archer-Antiquaries* he promoted the academic study of
everything pertaining to archery, but in particular to that of the
composite bow.

Of equal inspiration and assistance has been Lukas Novotny, a
composite bowyer and horse-archer of distinction. I thank him for
allowing me to spend time at his workshop, photographing him
building bows, for the magnificent bows he has made for me and for
everything he has taught me about horse-archery and the composite
bow in general. He is always very generous with his knowledge.

Robert Molineaux belongs to a new generation of archer-
antiquary scholars and is also a fine maker of composite bows. I
am deeply indebted to him for creating the line drawings that
populate the typology in the following pages and also for his
erudite input.

Justin Ma and Peter Dekker, eminent scholars in the field,
deserve special mention. They have been unstinting in sharing
their encyclopaedic knowledge and in reading sections of the text.
Thanks are also due to Stephen Selby, Adam Karpowicz, Wendy
Hodgkinson, David Joseph Wright, Gökmen Altinkulp, Cemal
Hünal, Jaap Koppedrayer, Han Zhang and Annette Bächstädt
who have all helped in various ways. I am enormously grateful to
my wife, Kim Hawkins, for taking so many excellent
photographs for the book, as well as for her unflagging support.

My sincere thanks also go to Nathalie Guion and Hilary
Merrill at the Sonoma Coastal EquesTraining Center, who
welcomed me warmly when I proposed the idea of a horse-
archery club – the California Centaurs. Finally a salute to
Valkyrie, the horse who stole my heart.

Artist's note

Readers may care to note that the original paintings from which
the artwork plates in this book were prepared are available for
private sale. All reproduction copyright whatsoever is retained by
the Publishers. All enquiries should be addressed to:

Peter Dennis, 'Fieldhead', The Park, Mansfield, Nottinghamshire
NG18 2AT, UK, or email magie.h@ntlworld.com

The publishers regret that they can enter into no correspondence
upon this matter.

Editor's note

Measurements are given using the imperial scale, which has the
following approximations on the metric scale:

1 mile = 1.6km
1 yard = 0.9m
1 foot = 0.3m
1 inch = 25.4mm
1lb = 0.45kg

CONTENTS

INTRODUCTION

Shooting a composite bow with traditional techniques is a dynamic and thrilling form of archery. It is done with flair, punch and attack. It is done standing, kneeling, walking, running; it is done from the platform of thundering chariots and from the back of galloping horses. The materials – wood, horn, sinew – sing in the hand; their oscillations in tune with the body. Composite bows are smooth to draw, both because of their cleverly engineered designs and because of the perfect elasticity of these components. A true horn-and-sinew composite bow is a superior bow.

Across the epochs and empires of the Eastern and Near Eastern world, composite bows have appeared in a diverse array of sculptural forms – beautiful shapes that change dramatically through the various stages of being strung and drawn. To protect the component materials from the weather, composite bows often had coverings of either bark or leather; they were then frequently painted with opulent decoration before being

This quartet of composite bows in Peter Dekker's collection illustrates just some of its diverse forms. From top down: Korean bow, Mughal crab bow, Ottoman war bow, Qing bow (note that the string bridges are missing on this specimen). These bows vary considerably both in size and shape and were designed to shoot a correspondingly diverse range of arrows, varying in weight, dimension and style of arrowhead. Some bows, such as the Korean bow, were built for speed and distance, shooting light arrows rapidly; while others, such as the Qing bow, were engineered to deliver a very long, heavy arrow. To the Manchu (Qing Dynasty) heavyweight punch and accuracy were more important than either rate of shooting or great distance. (Photograph courtesy of Peter Dekker)

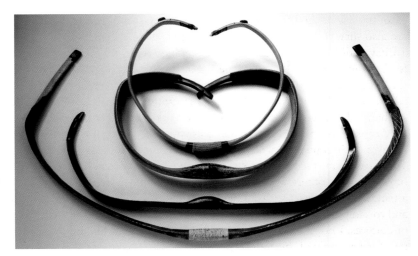

sealed with a lacquer. Composite bows were not only highly efficient weapons; they were also exquisite works of art.

According to the *Encyclopaedia of Archery* a composite bow is 'composed of three or more layers of dissimilar materials' (Paterson 1984: 38). This distinguishes it from a self bow, which is one that is made from a single homogenous material, such as a wooden bow from yew or elm and a laminated bow, which Paterson, a respected authority, defines as 'a bow constructed from several layers of basically similar materials' (Paterson 1984: 73). The Japanese *yumi* is constructed from laminations of bamboo and deciduous wood (usually mulberry wood) and is therefore classed as a laminated bow. Discussion of its bold proportions, asymmetric elegance and gracious curves will have to await a future volume, for it is not a true composite bow.

A bow is a spring. Bending the limbs stores elastic potential energy, which is then released when the bow is shot. The heavier the draw-weight of the bow, the more energy is generated. However, the efficiency of composite-bow materials and design meant that less effort had to be expended for a performance equivalent to that of a self or laminated bow. An English longbow, for example, would need to be of significantly higher draw-weight to launch an arrow of the same weight and dimensions at the same speed.

Composite bows were high-status weapons – they were expensive. Manufacture required highly developed skills and took a long time. The glues used to bond the sinew and horn were slow to dry, and a composite bow was at least several months in the making. In fact there is a correlation between how long a bow was left to dry and set in a pre-stressed shape before moving to the next stage of manufacture and the resultant power of that bow. The strongest bows took one or even two years to produce, and that gave them considerable value.

Despite their expense, composite bows were used in large numbers, both by regiments of infantry archers and massed troops of horse-archers. Even so, this widespread employment did nothing to diminish the high standing of the composite bow among warrior elites – it remained the aristocratic weapon of choice.

Medieval treatises on *furūsiyya* – the Arabic knightly arts of war – extol the use of the bow on horseback as the most noble of skills. There are also surviving manuscripts from various Chinese dynasties, Ottoman Turkey, India and Persia, among others, which offer practical instruction for both infantry- and horse-archers. Their existence is an indicator that the upper echelons of the composite-bow-archer class were, in large part, educated and literate. It is not until 1545, with the publication of Roger Ascham's *Toxophilus*, that an equivalent work was available in the West.

Arabs, Assyrians, Avars, Chinese, Egyptians, Hittites, Huns, Koreans, Magyars, Mongols, Mughals, Parthians, Persians, Scythians, Tartars and Turks are among the chief peoples to have used and venerated the composite bow. There are others, spanning both time and continent, and all jostle for attention. In this brief survey it is only possible to touch on a few themes and to sample just some of the practices and archery lore from such a span of cultures. I hope, though, that it will be enough to stimulate the reader into further study of this most fascinating and bewitching of arms.

The main driver for different bow designs was the type of arrow they were intended to launch. To illustrate the extremes of arrow design that have informed the requirements of bow design, this image shows a replica Qing arrow (manufactured by Jaap Koppedrayer) alongside a Turkish flight arrow (author's collection). (KH)

DEVELOPMENT
Engineering the optimal bow

GEOMETRY

There are two essential elements to a composite bow – the geometry and the materials. To begin with the geometry: bow-limbs that bend away from the archer are known as reflex and those that bend towards the archer are known as deflex. A combination of reflex and deflex is called a recurve. Composite bows appear in a variety of forms but they are all, to a greater or lesser extent, recurve bows. There is a trade-off of benefits between reflex and deflex, and the search for the perfect bow led to an extraordinary diversity in bow designs.

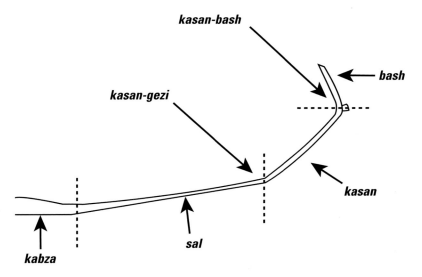

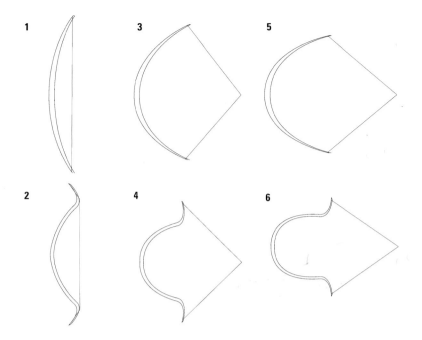

Here we see a mechanical difference between a straight-limbed bow (**1**) and a recurve bow (**2**). Above centre, we see a straight-limbed bow drawn to its optimal point for bending (**3**). This is the limit of this bow's mechanical efficiency, although it is not necessarily at full draw. Below centre, we see a recurve bow drawn to an equivalent length (**4**). Here the limbs retain considerable potential for bending beyond this point and the siyahs are about to come into play to assist that further bend. Above right, we see the straight-limbed bow pulled beyond its optimal bending curve (**5**) where the limbs are now being stretched rather than bent. Below right, we see the recurve bow drawn to an equivalent length (**6**) where the rigid siyahs continue to work as levers to lessen the work required to flex the bending section, demonstrating both the greater efficiency and the longer draw of the recurve design. (Drawings by Robert J. Molineaux)

One distinct advantage of a recurve bow is that the design, combined with the powerfully elastic properties of the materials, induces the limbs to return with an accelerating velocity; this in turn transfers into arrow speed. To deliver an equivalent performance with a non-recurve self-bow would require a heavier draw-weight. Secondly, a recurve design requires less work from the archer to draw the bow to its full extent. When drawing a bow, the ends of the bow (the *kasan* and *bash* sections and, where present, the *siyahs*) do not bend, but rather act as levers. With a relatively straight-limbed bow such as the longbow, for example, there comes a point where the tips pass an optimal angle and no longer offer mechanical advantage to bending the limbs. At this point the archer perceives an increase in the effort required to draw the bow, a phenomenon known as stacking. It feels harder to pull, yet there has been no actual increase in either power or draw-weight. Once the tips cease to act as levers, the archer is in effect trying to stretch the limbs rather than to bend them. By changing the angle of the energy transfer, the recurve limbs of a composite bow, acting like crowbars, permit the archer to draw a bow of comparable draw-weight for significantly less muscular exertion.

Contact recurve bows, having long *siyahs* that sweep away from the archer, offered an additional advantage to the archer – 'let-off'. Although he had to push through an initial resistance at the commencement of the draw, as the levers reached the appropriate angle, he would feel a distinct let-off in draw-weight. This in turn enabled him to hold at full draw for longer. The downside of this design was that with beefed-up *siyahs* and string bridges, there was an addition of mass to the limb: mass that required energy to shift – energy that would otherwise have been transferred to the arrow. With a non-contact recurve bow, there remained some degree of lever advantage; and because the angle was

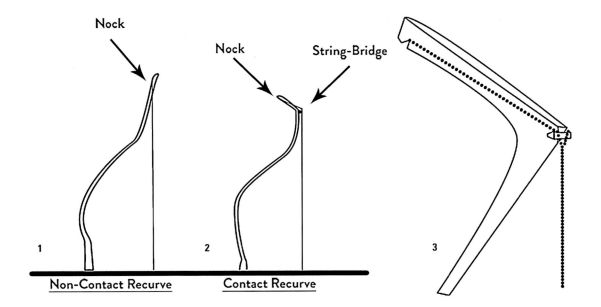

Nock

Nock **String-Bridge**

1

2

3

Non-Contact Recurve   **Contact Recurve**

One further aspect of geometry to be noted is the distinction between non-contact (**1**) and contact (**2**) recurve bows. On some bow designs, particularly those with highly reflexed *siyahs* – that is, pointing away from the archer – the string comes into contact with the bow at the upper end in the resting position and if left unmodified, it would have a tendency to slip off. Obviously, there is a requirement for the string to form a taut and straight line. The remedy was to affix a block, usually of horn, wood or bone at the junction between *kasan* and *siyah*. This was known as a string bridge (**3**) or string pad, depending on its prominence. On a Qing bow, for instance, the bridge needed to be quite large, whereas on a Turkish or Korean bow only a small pad was required to seat the string correctly. (Drawing by Robert J. Molineaux)

more torsionally stable, the *siyahs* could be made thinner and lighter, which enabled a more efficient energy transfer to the arrow. Every design modification in the composite bow's many manifestations had both advantages and consequences.

ORIGINS

The discovery of the advantages offered by a recurve design may have coincided with the early adoption of composite materials. Adding a sinew backing to strengthen a wooden bow seems the most likely first step; sinew's value as a strong and elastic material was well understood by early peoples. Many Native American bows were made with wood and a sinew backing alone. Compared to wood fibres, sinew fibres have a greater capacity to stretch before breaking, and the back of a bow (the part facing away from the archer) stretches the fibres a great deal on bending. Moreover, the sinew is applied wet in an adhesive solution and it shrinks as it dries. This shrinkage compresses the wood fibres so that they in turn are also more resilient to being pulled apart under tension. As the drying sinew shrinks it also pulls the tips of the bow away from the archer and creates a basic reflex design.

Sinew-backed bows with their higher tolerance of tensile failure enabled shorter bows to be made. This was especially useful in areas where long billets of suitably elastic bow-woods (such as yew or elm) were not available. Even where such woods were available – the North American West Coast, for instance – shorter, sinew-backed bows were widely used, possibly because hunters seeking concealment in low brush preferred them and because they offered greater power and general toughness.

Simple composites of wood and sinew produced very serviceable bows, but the next step was to enhance the power of the limbs by adding

horn. Shorter bows were particularly suited to this improvement because continuous strips of horn, whether from water buffalo, bighorn sheep or mountain goats, are limited in size. The inherent 'springiness' of horn, especially its ability to store energy under compression, made it the ideal material to complement the tensile strength of sinew. However, the essential advance that enabled the genesis of true composite bows was the discovery of the right types of glue. Only hide and fish glues have the strength and pliability to bond the sinew, and the horn, to a wooden core. The elasticity of these glues also contributes to the overall spring and resilience of composite bows. (Exceptionally, some Inuit bows have the sinew bound to the wooden core with an elaborate knot system because of the difficulties of manufacturing appropriate glues in extremely cold temperatures.)

Although the wooden core remained important to hold the bow in shape, in particular resisting torque, and although it continued to assist in the delivery of elastic power, its main function was to act as a framework for the shape of the bow. With everything held in place by multiple layers of sinew, the wooden core was able to take on elaborate shapes created by a series of joins. It could therefore be used to build engineered geometries that would optimize the potential energy created by the horn, the sinew and the wood when under strain.

The author with his replica of a Klamath Valley Native American bow, which has a magnificent piece of yew at its core. Built by Robert Molineaux, it was based on finds from the Klamath River Valley. Note how the sinew backing has pulled the limbs into reflex. The sinew has been painted to seal it from the damaging effects of moisture. Unstrung, it is only 40 inches from nock to nock, but its broad limbs and the sinew backing allow it to be drawn without breaking. It packs a punch of around 50lb, even though it can only be drawn to about 20 inches. A shorter draw is common with many aboriginal cultures. Expert stalking skills enabled the hunter to get extremely close to his prey and a short draw minimized movement so as not to startle the animal. (KH)

TYPOLOGY OF COMPOSITE BOWS

The diversity of historical composite-bow designs is vast, and space only permits a brief summary of some of the more predominant types.

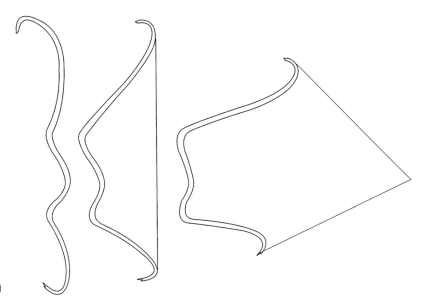

No other bow embodies both extremes of reflex and deflex to quite the same extent as the Scythian bow. According to the Greek historian Herodotus (5th century BC) the Scythians were a nomadic people, originating in central Persia, who migrated into the North Caucasus, Crimea and Black Sea regions. By the early centuries AD, the designation of Scythian ethnicity had become both broad and vague, encompassing a variety of peoples who inhabited the Pontic-Caspian Steppe. Celebrated as expert horse-archers with composite bows, the Scythians spread their influence – and their bows – even further afield. They reached West as far as the Danube, Indo-Scythians populated the Punjab region of North-West India and, to the East, their material artefacts have been found in areas of China adjacent to the silk routes. (Drawing by Robert J. Molineaux)

The Scythian bow

The Scythian bow lays claim to be one of the earliest types of fully composite bow, and it remained in use for many centuries. It is an extraordinary and elaborate construction of opposing curves that was once thought to be the product of artists' fanciful imaginations. During the first decade of the 21st century, however, archaeologists unearthed a number of bows, including one almost completely intact example, from graves in the Yanghai cemetery, Xinjiang, China. This magnificent bow is approximately 3,000 years old and reveals the same sinewy contours of a type of bow represented widely in Greek art. It was a Scythian bow.

In 2009 a magnificent working replica of the Yanghai bow was constructed by Adam Karpowicz. It was based on measurements and analysis by Stephen Selby, who had inspected the original at first hand. The bow possessed a central core formed by a continuous strip of horn in each limb, sandwiched between laths of wood, each approximately 6 inches in length and spliced to its fellow. The laminated core has a triangular cross-section, with the apex facing the belly of the bow. Fillets of wood were then applied to build out the bow along its length, creating a slightly more rounded cross-section before applying the sinew layer to the back of the bow. The whole was then wrapped in sinew and covered with a protective layer of birch bark. Among excavated samples there is some variation to the internal construction methodology, but all have a closely similar overall length and external shape.

It has not to date been possible to verify the precise type of wood or horn used in the original, though the wood is believed to have been tamarisk. Water buffalo horn was used for building the replica, but Selby and Karpowicz have speculated that it may have been the natural curl of the horn from the Siberian ibex that endowed the Scythian bow with its idiosyncratic shape (Selby & Karpowicz 2010: 94–102). If this is so, as seems probable, it begs the question as to whether the highly complex

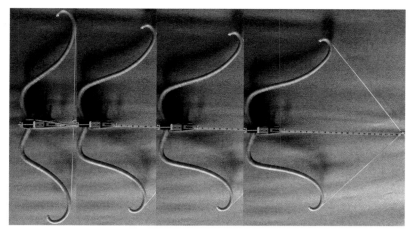

form of the Scythian bow was informed entirely by mechanical principles, or whether there was some belief in the shamanic power of the ibex. Certainly the ibex, along with the sturgeon (from which the best possible glue can be made for bonding the sinew) is prevalent in Scythian art, and it may have been thought that a weapon that embodied its mighty horns in some way took on some of its power.

The angular bow

It is possible that the Scythian style was the first type of composite bow, but there is another contender. In contrast to the sinuous serpentine curvature of the Scythian bow is the stark, linear geometry of the angular

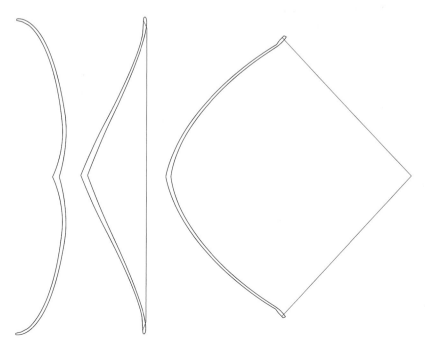

Replica Scythian bow, by Adam Karpowicz, showing the dramatic changes in profile as the bow is drawn. It has a draw-weight of 120lb at 28 inches. This shorter draw of the Scythian bow is often seen in art. However, arrows found alongside the original bow measured between 30 and 31 inches, indicating the possibility of a longer draw. Selby and Karpowicz calculate that the range of draw-weights for the Scythian bow would probably fall between 80lb and 140lb, comparable to estimates for other types of composite bow (Selby & Karpowicz 2010: 94–102). When considering draw-weights, it should be noted that the Scythian bow was also the bow of the 'Amazons', those celebrated warrior women who so terrified the Ancient Greeks with their horse-archery skills. Though undoubtedly a match for any man with their riding, shooting and ferocity, it may be that they used bows with draw-weights at the lower end of the scale. However, for the horse-archer, who can ride close to his target, this would not be a disadvantage. (Photograph courtesy of Stephen Selby)

In its unstrung mode, the angular bow resembles a very flattened 'W'; note the very pronounced deflex angle at the grip. When the angular bow is strung, the limbs assume the familiar triangular shape seen in art of the region, though it should be noted that there is more curve in the limbs and reflex at the tips than some of the cruder representations in art would suggest. When the angular bow is drawn fully, a little bit of archery magic occurs as the bow morphs yet again, forming a perfect crescent. The acute deflex angle at the grip facilitates the extremely long draw – the draw-hand reaching to the right shoulder – that we see in art depicting these bows. There are advantages to a long draw, just as there are to a longer barrel on a gun – the propelling force of the string acts on the arrow for a more sustained period. (Drawing by Robert J. Molineaux)

This replica angular bow, in the author's collection, was made by Lukas Novotny of Saluki Bow. The birch bark covering protects the sinew from the elements. It is a fast and powerful bow. Exceptionally light in the hand, despite its 75lb draw-weight, it is easy to manoeuvre. I have shot it on foot, from chariots and from horseback. Angular bows have especially narrow limbs, less than an inch wide before the bark wrap is applied, which means that they are vulnerable to torsion. When I first took delivery of my angular bow, I had a number of alarming moments as it sprung out of my hand. It turned itself inside out when attempting to string it or loosing it. It did this with a mighty and terrifying force! The problem was that I didn't have the bracing height set correctly. Bracing height is the distance between the centre of the string and the centre of the bow when strung in the resting position. Small adjustments can be made by twisting the string to shorten or lengthen it. Angular bows require a higher-than-average bracing height in order to hold the limbs under the correct tension to be stable. It was in an attempt to redress this stability problem that these bows have such an accentuated deflex at the grip; it helps to direct the limbs to bend in the correct alignment. (KH)

bow. Developed in the Ancient Near East, this is the type of bow that is represented universally in art from Mesopotamia to Anatolia and, most significantly, evidenced in surviving specimens of actual bows; notably those from the tomb of Tutankhamun. It is generally accepted that the angular bow was introduced into Egypt by the Hyksos at some point during the 17th century BC. The Hyksos probably originated from somewhere in the Levant. The angular bow became the bow of choice for Egyptians, Hittites and Assyrians and many others in the region. It was the universal bow for the chariot-archer and, with the Assyrians, transferred to be the arm of the horse-archer. As an infantry weapon it was employed both on the battlefield and in siege warfare.

At first glance, viewed when strung but not yet drawn, the angular bow appears to be a most unlikely shape for a bow. The steep angle at the centre gives the impression that the bow is already starting to break. However, it is in fact an excellent bow. Neither the horn nor the sinew have joins at the apex of the angle – both run in continuous strips through the angle in laminated overlays. Moreover, the grip comes under relatively little load when the entire bow is flexing.

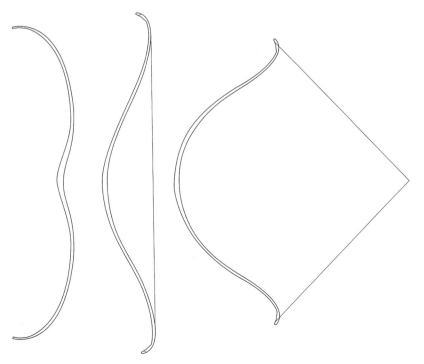

The bow of the Achaemenid Persians combined the simple lines of the angular bow with the sinuous elegance of the Scythian bow. Sufficiently reflexed to offer exceptionally high-speed limb return with elongated tips that provided efficient leverage for a powerful draw and sufficiently deflexed at the grip section to accommodate a long draw, this was a beautifully designed bow. (Drawing by Robert J. Molineaux)

The Achaemenid bow

The Achaemenid Empire, known also as the First Persian Empire (*c*.550–330 BC), was founded by Cyrus the Great and became the largest empire in the Ancient World. It employed masses of infantry archers in its armies, the scourge of the Greek city-states. This is the bow of the famed 'Immortals', a select force of 10,000 men who served as elite infantry on the battlefield and also as the Imperial Guard. It was also a bow that was put to good use by horse-archers.

The Turkish bow

Under Ottoman rule, archery was practised in every city, town and village, archery literature abounded and archers of merit were held in the highest esteem. This was so in other composite-bow cultures, but perhaps nowhere was archery quite as venerated as it was in the realms of the Ottoman Turks. Being able to shoot the furthest distance became a national obsession, and they took bow design to new frontiers. There were two main types of Ottoman Turkish bow – the *hilal kuram* bow and the *tekne kuram* bow. Each shape achieves a different goal by varying the length of the limbs, adjusting the curve and setting the stiffness of the *kasan-gezi*.

Hilal kuram bows were designed for flight-shooting – an activity that enjoyed great popularity as an aristocratic sport in Ottoman Turkey and which was concerned solely with the distance an arrow can be shot – and had the ability to cast very light arrows a very great distance. I own two, both made by the master bowyer Lukas Novotny. This is not a novice bow, though I was a novice when I acquired mine. Suffice to say that when things go wrong, as they do with such a virtuoso instrument, the epithet 'temperamental' is not exclusive to the bow. Even so, I find these bows astonishingly beautiful; they have taught me a great deal, and I enjoy shooting them immensely. As I draw them, I never cease to be thrilled by their dramatic changes in shape and the extraordinary power of such a feather-light object.

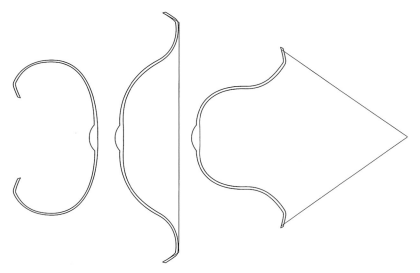

The *hilal kuram* or 'crescent moon shape' bow is short with slender limbs, and is extremely reflexed – characteristics that reduce its mass, enhancing the speed of limb return – but at the cost of making it less stable. By having a long, continuous transition between the *sal* and the *kasan* sections, which remained stiff in all stages of the bend, the *hilal kuram* bow bent in an arc closer to the central grip than was common in other bows. This increased the bow's mechanical efficiency but further reduced its stability. The result is a bow that can be temperamental but with a cast that is unparalleled. (Drawing by Robert J. Molineaux)

The *tekne kuram* or 'boat shape' bow was designed for both warfare and target archery. Wider-limbed and less reflexed than the *hilal kuram* bow, the *tekne kuram*, most importantly, had a moderately bendable *kasan-gezi*. This subtle and supple flex in the *kasan-gezi* offered advantages to a bow that had to withstand the rigours of campaign, albeit at the expense of some mechanical efficiency. It made the bow more stable and much less likely to turn inside out. Moreover, *tekne kuram* bows could, if necessary, be left strung for extended periods of time, because the stresses were distributed over wider and longer limbs. (Drawing by Robert J. Molineaux

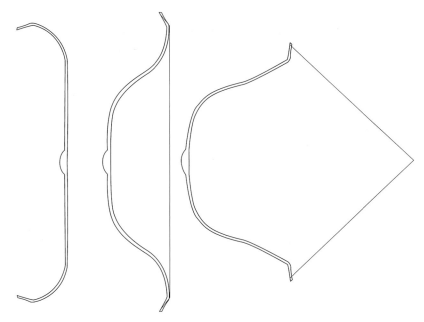

In addition to these two main types, there were other Turkish bows, including one called the *kepade*, which was a light draw-weight, slightly reflexed bow, used exclusively for practising form. It had a padded section on the string and the tyro used it with a three-finger draw for conditioning. Mustafa Kani, a Turkish master who wrote a treatise on

The explosive power of the Turkish bow is evident in these two images of *hilal kuram* bows, both made by Lukas Novotny. Note the extreme reversal of the curve of the limbs from the resting to the strung state. Tremendous forces are at work here. (KH)

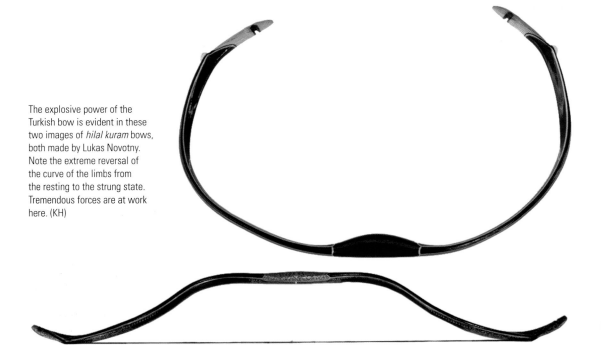

archery in 1847, commands the novice to be able to draw it 500 times in succession without tiring. As if this were not daunting enough, he adds 'it is altogether advantageous if he can draw it 30,000 times' (quoted in Klopsteg 1987: 111). Further, Kani stipulates that all archers, whatever their level of experience and no matter how busy they are with other matters, should draw the practice bow 66 times every morning upon rising throughout their lives. (66 is a number of religious significance to Muslims.)

The back and sides of Turkish bows, where the sinew was exposed, were covered with fine leather and sealed with varnish, usually sandarac. This not only protected the sinew from the warping effects of moisture but it also provided a reasonably rugged outer skin to withstand the knocks and bumps of military life. These leather facings also provided a canvas for the most exquisitely painted and gilded arabesque decoration. When combined with similar ornament on the highly polished surface of the horn belly, this created bows of exceptional beauty.

The Mughal crab bow

Closely allied to the Turkish *hilal kuram* is the *kaman* or crab bow of Mughal India. This remarkable bow took recurve design and the properties of composite materials to the extreme. In some examples the tips, in the unstrung state, curl so acutely towards the centre that they overlap, resembling the pincers of a crab.

Unlike the *hilal kuram*, however, the limbs of the crab bow are wide, allowing the bow to be left strung for extended periods of time. This was often desirable because the process of stringing and unstringing such a bow could be both exhausting and somewhat perilous. The broader limbs also meant that it didn't quite have the ultimate performance of its slender Turkish cousin.

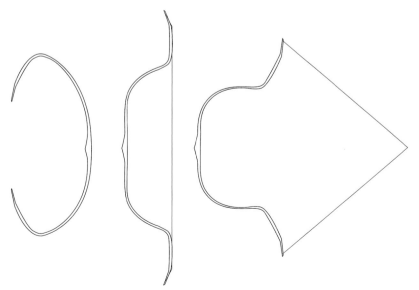

Crab bows place an enormous amount of reflex into the bow's *kasan-gezi* and a small amount in the transition between the *kasan* and *bash*. Both of these reflex points are then left completely stiff and non-flexible, forcing the entire bend in to the working limbs alone. The result is a bow that at full draw pushes the ends of the working limbs past the point of being parallel to each other! (Drawing by Robert J. Molineaux)

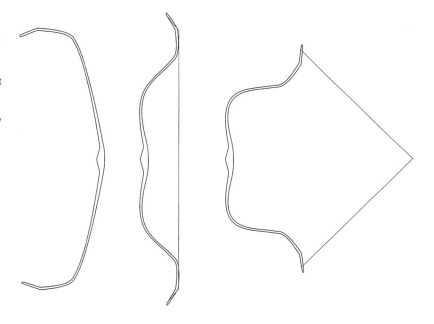

The working sections of the Indo-Persian bow are wider and longer than those of Ottoman war bows, while the *kasan* and *bash* sections are shorter. This results in a stable bow that is fast and also capable of delivering a heavier war arrow than its Ottoman counterpart. (Drawing by Robert J. Molineaux)

An Indo-Persian bow in the collections of the Pitt Rivers Museum, Oxford. Note the broad limbs. The back of the bow has been exquisitely painted with scenes from the hunt. (© Pitt Rivers Museum, University of Oxford)

The Indo-Persian bow

Widely used both on the battlefield and in the chase was the Indo-Persian bow. Unlike Ottoman bows, which were typically built with a three-piece wooden core construction, Indo-Persian bows usually consist of a five- or even seven-part wooden core. Their simpler, elegant external form masks an intricate level of engineering within. Moreover, the breathtaking magnificence of their painted and gilded surface decoration is a match for even the finest Ottoman bow. While Ottoman bows are decorated exclusively in intricate scrolling and floral patterns, Indo-Persian bows often feature delightful figurative painting.

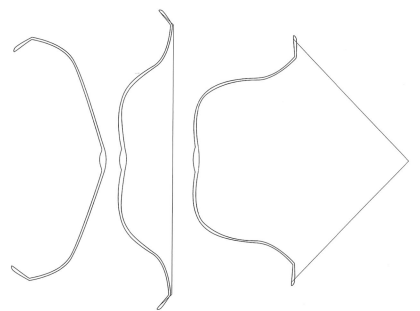

Most significantly, the Crimean Tatar bow possesses *siyahs*. Similar to the *bash*, in that they are a non-bending tip to the bow, *siyahs* are much longer wooden extensions adjoining the *kasan*. They accentuate the mechanical assistance given to the archer in pulling back the limbs; they are levers. In particular, they facilitate the use of a long draw and a heavy draw-weight. The Crimean Tatar bow was well suited to shooting a lengthy war-arrow of considerable mass. (Drawing by Robert J. Molineaux)

The Crimean Tatar bow

Even though they were substantially longer, Crimean Tatar bows were constructed using methods closely similar to those used to manufacture Ottoman Turkish bows. The Crimean Tatars were an integral part of the Ottoman military, and Ottoman bowyers regularly produced their native style of bows to satisfy military demand in that region. Crimean Tatar bows had long working limbs and, often, a deeply reflexed grip. The transition into the *kasan* at the *kasan-gezi* was much less acute than in shorter bows, and the *kasan* itself takes up less of the bow's length proportionally when compared to Ottoman bows.

The Magyar/Hun bow

The principal materials of composite bows – horn, wood, sinew – decompose readily. Consequently, there is a scarcity of excavated evidence for most types of composite bow. Exceptions to this are the bows of the Huns and Magyars – twin branches of what may be broadly thought of as the same peoples. Their bows used plates of bone as side panels to stiffen both the grip and the *siyahs*, and bone survives very well in almost any soil condition. It was the practice of these peoples to bury a warrior with his bow laid across his chest. Numerous graves, from Siberia to Western Europe, have been unearthed with the bone plates *in situ* and intact. This has enabled precise and reliable calculations to be made for the size and shape of the original bows. The *siyahs* on a Hun bow were angled to correct twist in the working limbs. Although not the most efficient of composite bows, this type was among the most user-friendly and received widespread use with peoples living a rugged outdoor life.

The Hun bow is a powerful, robust, medium-sized bow with long *siyahs*. Although it is most associated with the area that is now Hungary and it achieved its greatest military distinction in the marauding armies of Attila, it should perhaps be considered more of a pan-Eurasian bow, as its geographical dispersal was very wide. It is essentially an old Turkic steppe design that may lay claim to be one of the longest in continuous use. (Drawing by Robert J. Molineaux)

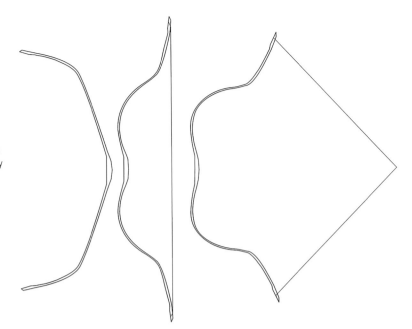

The asymmetric Hun bow

A variation of the regular Hunnic bow, which also had the grip and *siyahs* stiffened with bone plates, was one with asymmetric configuration. The mechanical benefits of asymmetric design are hotly debated among bowyers, but the arguments are too lengthy and technical to consider here. One theory is that it was a way of providing a bow with considerable draw-length and power – a long bow – while maintaining the lower limb as short as possible for convenient use on horseback.

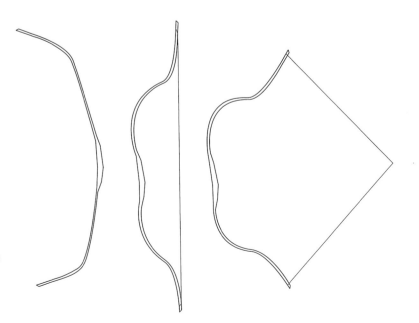

The asymmetric Hun bow has the upper limb longer than the lower limb – a feature it shares with the Japanese *yumi*. (Drawing by Robert J. Molineaux)

18

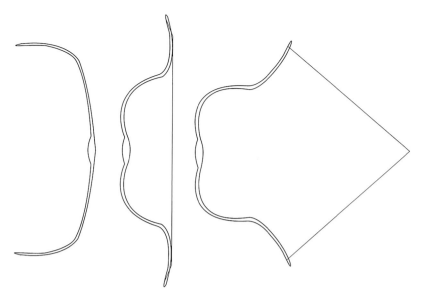

The Mongolian bow

By the 17th century the Mongols had all but abandoned use of the bow in warfare. Their principal adversaries, the Manchu (Chinese Qing Dynasty, 1644–1912), were the last major culture to continue the use of the bow as a mainstream weapon. It was only after the fall of the Dzungar Khanate (1758) that the bow, in the form of the Qing bow, was reintroduced into Mongolian martial culture.

The drawing here represents a bow of the Genghis Khan (Conquest) period. It is based upon a bow found, still strung, in a cave at Tsagaan Khad, Mongolia, dated to the 14th century, and upon bows depicted in contemporary paintings. Images in art show bows that were relatively short with broad limbs. They had long, sweeping *siyahs* and a prominent semi-triangular *kasan* section that provided the necessary structural strength between the accelerating forward angle of the nocks and the acute reflex of the bending limbs. The Tsagaan Khad bow showed traces of delicate decoration with red, black and yellow pigment, gold leaf, and birch bark inlays. It also possessed a red silk string. The bows that are in common use in Mongolia today are in fact a slightly smaller variant of the Qing bow. They are not bows that would have been familiar to Genghis Khan or his successors in the 13th century. (Drawing by Robert J. Molineaux)

The Korean bow

The Choson Dynasty dominated the Korean peninsula for five centuries (1392–1897), and archery flourished under its influence, achieving both

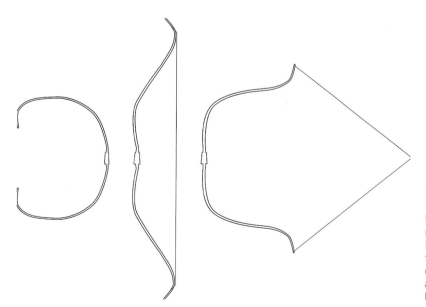

Similar in many ways to the Ottoman flight bow, the Korean bow was designed for extreme performance. Examples of older Korean war bows show that the limbs were originally wider, offering the necessary stability for a battlefield weapon. (Drawing by Robert J. Molineaux)

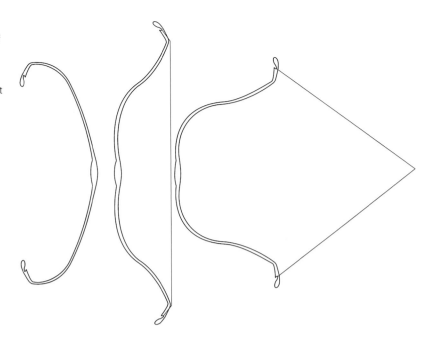

While most bowyers use a tree wood for the core, the builders of Ming bows favoured seasoned bamboo, and Gao Ying goes into considerable detail about the various stages of preparation that are necessary for this material. He also specifies where the best horn, sinew and glues are to be obtained and recommends mulberry for the *siyahs* (Tian & Ma 2015: 75–77). (Drawing by Robert J. Molineaux)

a military and cultural high status. The Korean bow is a very fast bow that embodies an astounding amount of spring and elasticity, resulting in phenomenal cast. Its very narrow, fine limbs and its high degree of reflex render it prone to twisting and reversing, however, and it requires constant and expert tuning and maintenance.

The Ming bow

Archery was valued very highly indeed in the military culture of the Ming Dynasty (1368–1644); it played a central role on the battlefield, in the hunt and in the lavish military spectacles of the Ming court. To date, there has been no excavated example of a Ming bow, nor have any survived in collections. Nevertheless there is no shortage of references in art, giving a clear idea of the various forms in common use. Moreover Gao Ying, writing in 1637 in his treatise *The Way of Archery*, fills in the gaps with detailed accounts of materials and construction techniques. He also cautions: 'When people these days choose bows, they pay attention to whether the outside is shiny and pretty. They do not realize the most critical element of the bow is the core, followed by the tips, then the horn, the sinew and lastly the glue' (quoted in Tian & Ma 2015: 75).

The Qing bow

The Qing or Manchu bow is the longest and most massive of all composite-bow types. It is a very impressive bow indeed. Qing bows favoured mulberry, or similar wood, as the core; bamboo cores were considered inferior. The Qing Dynasty (1644–1912), known also as the Manchu Dynasty, coincided with the age of firearms and the use of the

musket on the battlefield. Yet, for these fierce warriors from Manchuria, the bow retained a pre-eminent role both as an infantry and a cavalry weapon.

The Qing bow sits at the opposite end of the spectrum to the Turkish flight bow. It was the optimal design for shooting the heaviest and longest of arrows and delivering them with a hefty thump of kinetic energy. It was a bow for the power shot, rather than the rapid shot. Despite its great size, it was managed adroitly by Manchu horse-archers both on the battlefield and in the hunt and Manchu infantry archers were agile and nimble, often shooting on the move.

One sub-type of Qing bows that are of special interest are 'strength bows', sometimes known as 'numbered bows'. Larger than usual, these were broad-limbed bows of extra-heavy draw-weight, braced with a thick ox-gut string. Many, though not all, examples bore a wax seal stamped with a number. The number testified to the draw-weight of the bow, so that a No. 1 bow, for instance, had a draw-weight of just over 156lb and a No. 2 bow drew 130lb. Draw-weights did not necessarily descend uniformly with the bow's number, however, and there are references to some bows having a draw-weight as heavy as 240lb.

An 18th-century Qing bow in the collections of the Royal Armouries, Leeds. Remarkably, it is still able to be strung. It weighs 2lb 4oz and, when strung, measures 64.7 inches. Note the long *siyahs* and the staghorn string bridges. The back is covered with birch bark and the grip with cork. (© Royal Armouries XXIVB.40)

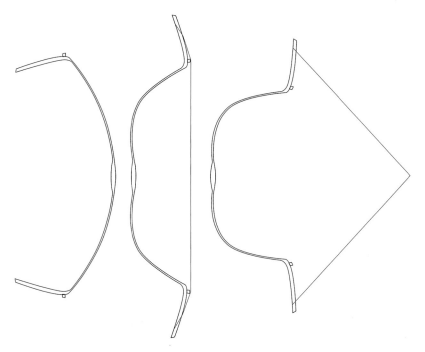

The Qing bow's large proportions were designed to propel an especially heavy arrow to deliver a thumping blow that, at short range, would more than match the impact of a musket ball. In order to do this the Qing bow was fitted with long *siyahs*, tremendously powerful levers that abutted to the bending section of the limbs at an extreme angle and via a short but very stout *kasan*, which provided an entirely stiff transition between the *siyah* and the bending limb. This configuration offered the capacity for an exceptionally long draw – Manchu archers drew all the way back to the point of the right shoulder – and very powerful draw-weights. (Drawing by Robert J. Molineaux)

Maple was considered the best wood for building the core of the bow. Note the straight grain, which helps to deter the bow from twisting. Maple was also favoured because it takes glue very well and both the lamination of the horn to the wood and the joins of the wooden core itself were dependent on the strength of adhesive bonds. (ML)

'Strength bows' were used during the archery component of a military examination to test a candidate's ability for drawing a heavy bow. They were never used for shooting arrows, merely as a measurement of an archer's might. The cadet extended his left arm and, holding the string with all four fingers, demonstrated, if he could, a full draw. He was obliged to perform the action three times. Such feats of strength were also accompanied by tests of shooting ability using regular bows.

MATERIALS AND MANUFACTURE

Materials

The *Tale of Aquat*, an Ugaritic text from the 14th century BC and originating from what is now Syria, has the following lines:

> I vow yew trees of Lebanon
> I vow sinews from wild oxen;
> I vow horns from mountain goats
> Tendons from the hocks of a bull
> I vow from a cane-forest reeds:
> Give these to Kothar wa-Khasis
> He'll make a bow for thee (Quoted in Pritchard 2011: 139)

It is a list of ingredients for a composite bow and its companion arrows. The precise species of materials varied according to region and period but all composite bows consisted of wood, horn, sinew and glue with either a bark or leather casing.

In general, maple has been the wood of choice for making the core, though there are mentions of yew in some Turkish texts. Not only does maple have a fine, straight grain and good elastic properties, it also bonds securely with adhesives: 'Maple accepts glue exceedingly well, and is one of the best-gluing of all cabinet woods' (Klopsteg 1987: 41). For the finest bows the tree has to be felled when growth is dormant, and a single bole of maple produces sufficient timber for only two bows (Klopsteg 1987: 42).

Horn from the water buffalo. This is the most widely used horn for composite bows, able to withstand compression and to store and release energy to an exceptional degree. Other types of horn can be used, though bovine horn tends to delaminate too easily. The horn is applied as a single continuous piece to each limb of the bow. It is sawn from the horn in longitudinal strips. These strips are steamed to soften them and, for uniformity, sometimes clamped against a flat iron bar while drying, in order to remove the curl. (ML)

Though Hun bows famously use the horn of Hungarian grey cattle (*Bos taurus*), the most universal horn used in the making of the composite bow was that of the water buffalo (*Bubalus bubalis*). This was readily available throughout the parts of the world that adopted the composite bow. One might think of the horn as the muscles of the bow and the wooden core as its skeleton. To extend this analogy, we must also think of the work done by the tendons in an animal body, and this is exactly the role provided by sinew in the composite bow. It is what holds it all together under tremendous strain and it also lends a great deal of elastic power to the flex and return of the limbs.

Animal sinew, when hammered and combed to reduce it to fine fibre strands, has phenomenal tensile strength. According to Klopsteg, reporting on a 19th-century Turkish work by Mustafa Kani, the best sinew came from the Achilles' tendon of cattle (Klopsteg 1987: 42). However, many present-day bowyers prefer the broader, longer and more fibrous backstrap tendon from cattle or deer, as well as tendon from the ostrich.

The broad, long tendons that extend along a quadruped's spine are known colloquially as 'backstrap tendon' and are usually sourced from cattle. They not only deconstruct readily into fine strands of sinew, but also produce especially long and strong fibres, which are ideal for applying to the back of the bow. After being hammered on a wooden block the sinew is worked by hand. Gradually, it is reduced to finer and finer fibres, which can then be combed and laid into neat bunches ready for applying to the bow. (ML)

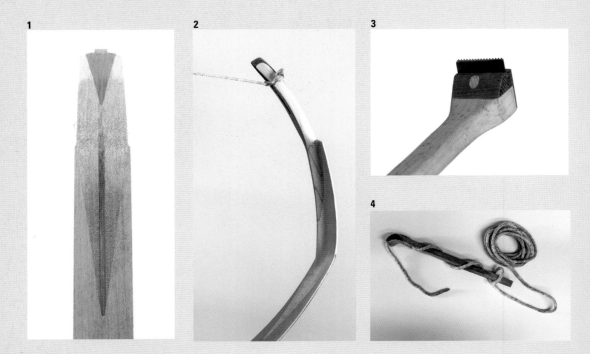

Building a bow

Once the materials have been prepared, the bowyer begins by making the wooden core (**1**). Billets of maple are steam-bent to create the all-important reflex of the bending section. Once set, these are joined to the other parts of the bow, which have been meticulously shaped with saw, chisel and file. Tendon glue and precision joints ensure the structural integrity of the wooden core. High-stress zones, such as the *kasan* and the *bash*, may also be reinforced with inserts of horn.

After the glue has dried, the wooden core is scraped and sanded into a smooth finished shape (**2**). Note the engineered strength of the *kasan* profile, which manages the stress of transferring the levered power from the *bash* into the reflex resistance of the *sal*. Both the core and the strips of horn to be applied to its belly are shaped to form a convex surface on one side of the wood that will seat snugly into a corresponding concave gutter on the horn. This concave/convex shaping also provides structural strength in the same way that a retractable steel tape measure is stiffened by its shape.

Both surfaces are also scraped using a tool called a *tashin* – a bowyer's scraper (**3**). This scores parallel, corrugated lines on both the wooden core and the horn strip that attaches to it. These grooves not only increase the surface area for the glue, but also increase resistance to sideways slip.

Tendon glue is then applied to affix a strip of horn to each limb, building the muscles of the bow. The lamination is held under pressure while it dries by means of a helically wound cord applied

with a tool called a *tendyek* (**4**). This tensioning tool enables him to create both a strong and even pressure with every turn. A cord is then tied between the nocks and tensioned with a peg. This holds the bow under reflex tension while drying and manipulates the limbs into alignment. The bow is then placed in a conditioning box.

Today, the conditioning box is an insulated container warmed by heat lamps (**5**), but it was formerly a felt-lined wooden box that was placed into a baking oven. Bows and bow parts were placed in an environment of steady warmth either while drying in manufacture or prior to tuning manipulation during their working life. In this example the conditioning box houses a pair of steam-bent strips of maple setting into their reflex shape while being clamped to formers. There is also a full core that has received its horn layers and is being left to dry – note the spiral of rope holding the lamination under pressure throughput its length.

When ready – and the longer it can be left to dry the better – a rasp is used to shape the horn on the back of the bow, tapering it into a smooth union with the core and determining an even thickness, according to desired draw-weight, along its length. Next the entire core is coaxed into a more finished shape with drawknife, rasp and abrasive papers. At the very centre of the bow, where the two plates of horn meet, is a narrow gap (**6**). A small sliver of bone, called a *chelik*, is inserted into this. It has no real practical function but it possesses a mystic significance.

The core is then ready to receive the sinew. This will both augment the power of the bow and also make it tough and resilient. Small bundles of prepared sinew are soaked in fish glue and laid

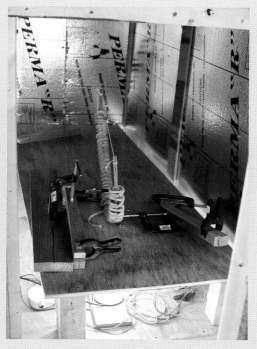

carefully onto the back of the bow (**7**). The sticky bundles of fibre have been dredged in a bath of gelatinous fish glue. Every strand must run straight; any snaking may cause twist in the finished bow. It is a critical and difficult task; it is an art. Much of it is accomplished with the bowyer's skilled and patient fingers but he also has a special tool, the *sinir kalemi* (**8**). Its teeth can be used to comb the sinew, its back can be used to smooth and flatten and the little hook is invaluable to tease out any snags. Made of brass and placed in a jar of water between applications, it resists becoming clogged with adhesive.

Strong bows require several layers of sinew, and each layer requires a drying time of several weeks. With each stage, the bowyer makes adjustments to the curvature and alignment of the limbs. Once the final layer of sinew has dried and the entire bow has been shaped and smoothed with abrasives, it is then tied, in extreme reflex, into a pretzel shape to season (**9**). Kani recommends that the best bows should be left in this state for about a year (Klopsteg 1987: 49). (All photos courtesy ML)

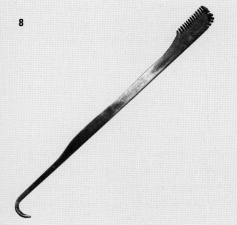

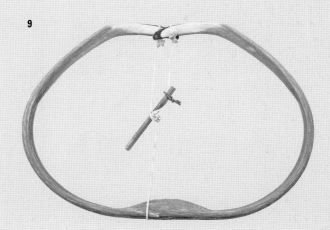

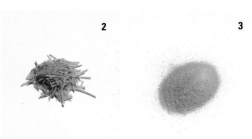

Leg tendons from cattle (**1**) were used to make the all-important glue that bonded the joins of the core and the lamination of the horn. According to Kani, the tendons were simmered in a solution of rainwater for several days. When cooled, the gelatinous mass was cut into strips and dried. A bowyer would then boil these strips in water to provide his daily supply (Klopsteg 1987: 40). Dried fish glue (**2**) was produced from either the swim bladders or the palate skin of fish, most desirably from that of the sturgeon. After drying, the material was shredded and then pounded into granules (**3**). These were boiled in solution and small swatches of sinew were then dredged in the glutinous liquid before being layed on the back of the bow. A particular advantage of fish glue was that it was slow drying, giving the bowyer time to perform his painstaking, detailed work. (ML)

The wood, the horn and the sinew all have to be held together by adhesives that remain secure under enormous stresses and are able to flex, stretch and contract without cracking. It is impossible to overstate the importance of the discovery of the correct glues in the development of the composite bow. Leg tendons were, and are still, used for making the glue that was used both to join the sections of the wooden core and also to bond the horn to that core. Hide glue was an acknowledged alternative, but tendon glue was the strongest. However, the application of the sinew required a different genus of adhesive – fish glue.

Tuning and stringing the bow

When released from its constraints the bow, now firmly set in an acute reflex, requires assistance to reverse the arc so that it can be strung. This is achieved with the aid of shaped wooden blocks, called *tepeliks*. The *tepeliks* tie to the bow, holding it in a semi-strung position while the fibres relax, before the bowyer puts a string on it for the first time.

Strings could be made from silk, but the anonymous author of *Arab Archery*, a 15th-century Arab treatise, recommends that the best strings should be made from 'the hide of a lean camel which has gone hungry through the winter and therefore has become emaciated', adding that in winter 'it should be rubbed with a fine polishing stone; then treated with a mixture of fox fat and yellow beeswax melted together' (Faris & Elmer 1945: 95). Strings were also made from goat hide, intestines or sinew. I have tested a sinew bowstring, well-waxed with beeswax, by soaking it in a tub of water for 24 hours. There was no indication of stretching and it shot perfectly well immediately afterwards.

Once strung, there then begins a wrestling match. The bowyer tunes the bow by bending it over his knees and by twisting and flexing it between his powerful hands. He adjusts the limbs correctively and holds them in position for a few minutes, encouraging them to take a new set. Working by eye, he alters any tendency a limb may have for torsion and he balances the tiller – by pushing an amount of curve from one limb, he induces correspondingly more curve in the other. It is strenuous work. Occasionally he will make slight adjustments by removing a bit of material with a scraper or smoothing with abrasives. He gradually pulls the bow to longer and longer draw-lengths, making careful adjustments every time he pulls it back another few inches. In some cases the bow may have to go back into the conditioning box to soften it prior to more strenuous manipulation. It is then shot repeatedly over days. With each arrow it is checked, corrected and tuned. When it is finally tamed, a protective leather covering can be glued over the sinew and the bow is handed to an archer. It remains a living thing, however, and that archer needs to know how to care for it and how to keep it fine-tuned.

Maintenance

There is a common misconception that composite bows were not popular in Western Europe because their performance would have been too adversely affected by the damp climate. However, when properly sealed, they not only thrived in the considerably wetter climes of Asia; composite bows, in the form of the bows for crossbows, proliferated throughout Europe. Social factors, military culture and economics were the reasons that composite bows did not see wider use in the West, not climate. Having said that, composite bows do require constant expert care and attention. They need to be shaded from direct sunlight just as much as they need to be kept warm and dry. Extreme changes in temperature can cause distortion or reduce performance.

Taybughā l-Ashrafī l-Baklamishī l-Yūnanī, author of *Kitāb ghunyat at-tullāb fī ma'rifat ramy an-nushshāb* ('Essential Archery for Beginners') *c.*1500, advises that when on campaign 'an archer should never neglect his bow for a single moment, and in extremes of temperature he should inspect it day and night, hour by hour, and not let it out of his mind even if he is sure that it is stable and true'. He continues, 'when the weather is cold, his best policy is to put the bow inside his clothes and warm it with his body. When going to bed at night, he should also keep the bow inside his clothes to protect it against the damp' (quoted in Latham & Paterson 1970: 94).

For more extreme twists, misalignments and tiller adjustments, Taybughā directs the archer to warm his bow gently by a fire before applying corrective pressures (Latham & Paterson 1970: 94). In *The Way of Archery* (1637), Gao Ying suggests that heating a bow over a fire before shooting is normal practice. This was presumably the case in colder climes (Tian & Ma 2015: 77). When yet more serious modifications are required, Taybughā recommends fixing the warmed bow into a rigid structure – some kind of mould or jig – which may be similar to the *tepeliks* used for the initial stringing of a new bow (Latham & Paterson 1970: 100). Such workshop hardware would presumably be stowed in the baggage train rather than carried by individual archers, but Taybughā clearly considered it part of every archer's remit to be able to undertake a sophisticated level of bow maintenance. Apart from their prowess at hitting the mark, this ability to maintain such a nuanced and expensive weapon is something that set these elite bowmen apart from other troops.

Although composite bows can remain strung for considerably longer than longbows without undue detriment, they do need to be unstrung and allowed to relax regularly or else they lose power. Images in art tend to show archers with only one bow but it is inconceivable that an archer depending on a composite bow in time of war would carry less than two. He must always have one strung in readiness for ambush or other surprise action and the second must rest in its unstrung state, preserving its power.

Of equal importance to care for the bow was maintenance of the bowstring, and 'having a second string to your bow' was an essential provision. According to one 16th-century Persian archery treatise, silk bowstrings should be changed every 40 days, or sooner if a lot of arrows have been shot (Khorasani 2013: 90).

Tepeliks tied to a previously unstrung bow. There is not only considerable resistance in reversing the extreme curve of the pretzel; it is also important that, at their first bending, the limbs suffer no twist. *Tepeliks* not only offer a pivot for leverage, they also provide a uniform curve, training the bow to its future bending pattern. (ML)

THE DEVELOPMENT OF SHOOTING TECHNIQUES

The thumb-draw

Alongside the mechanical developments of the bow came developments in the way the bow was drawn and loosed. For the composite bow, methods of drawing with the thumb were almost universal, although we see faint clues here and there of other techniques.

A thumb-draw is quite different from the so-called 'Mediterranean draw' of Western Europe, which hooks three (sometimes two) fingers around the string. This latter draw was used by longbowmen and remains the standard method today for archers with all types of bow. In the thumb-draw, usually accomplished with the aid of a thumb-ring, the string sits close to the crease of the thumb, which is folded around the string and secured in place by various combinations of the fingers.

The author of *Arab Archery* makes disparaging mention – 'a corrupt draw, used by the ignorant' – of a draw used by some Greeks who employed all four fingers on the string but no thumb (Faris & Elmer 1945: 45). Greek art certainly shows a number of methods. He also observes that: 'the Slavs have a peculiar draw which consists of locking the little finger, the ring finger and the middle finger on the string, holding the index finger outstretched along the arrow and completely ignoring the thumb ... They also make for their fingers *finger-tips* of gold, silver, copper and iron' (Faris & Elmer 1945: 45). This reference is reminiscent of a photograph from a private collection that appears in *Saracen Archery* (Latham & Paterson 1970: 136) of a pair of gold finger-tips that are purported to be Phoenician from the 5th century BC. Whatever the truth regarding the use of these idiosyncratic thimbles and other lesser known systems, there can be little doubt that some form of thumb-release was the norm for most users of the composite bow throughout history.

There are advantages to using the thumb to draw, whether with leather tab, glove or solid thumb-ring. One is that it makes it a great deal easier to hold a nocked arrow in place against the bow while moving; this is of significance because composite bows were used by a variety of archers who shot while in vigorous motion – from chariot-archers,

Lukas Novotny demonstrates a typical lock with a thumb-ring. *Arab Archery* (Faris & Elmer 1945: 43) gives six variations of lock for the thumb-draw, and there are yet others to be observed in the art of various cultures. (ML)

28

to horse-archers, to skirmishing infantry. All benefited by having more secure control of the arrow immediately prior to shooting.

In the three-finger draw, the fingers rotate the string clockwise, and it is partly for this reason that the arrow is placed against the left-hand side of the bow. To keep it in place the archer must keep the directional twist on the string and if necessary give the bow a slight diagonal tilt (known as canting the bow). However, when dealing with the bone-shaking bumps and bounces of a galloping chariot or the high-speed dash of a spirited horse, keeping the arrow against the bow becomes more challenging. With the thumb-draw, which places the arrow on the right-hand side of the bow, the index finger holds the arrow in place, however erratic the motion.

A further factor determining on which side of the bow the arrow should rest is the tendency of an arrow to flex as it is pushed forward by the string – aka archer's paradox. It bends around the bow as it leaves and, depending on whether the string has a clockwise twist (finger release) or an anti-clockwise twist (thumb-draw) it clears the bow more cleanly from the appropriate side.

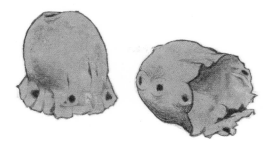

Modern illustration, based on an example in a private collection, of Phoenician finger-tips made from gold. The holes around the bases imply that they were sewn into a leather glove. Even so, it is very difficult to see how they might have aided a loose. It would be far too insecure to hold the string on just the tips of the fingers and it seems to me that they would interfere with a clean release if the string were held below them. To date they remain an intriguing and unsolved puzzle. (Illustration by David Joseph Wright)

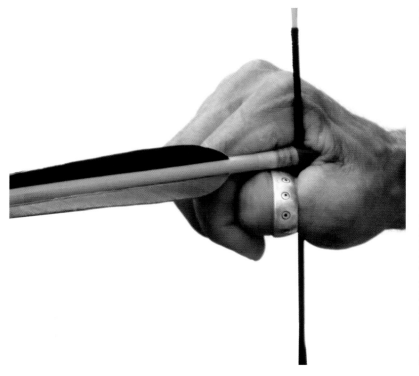

Lukas Novotny demonstrating how the lock of the thumb-draw holds the arrow securely against the bow at all stages of the draw. The thumb-release, which gives the string a clockwise rotation, is better served by placing the arrow on the right-hand side of the bow. This results in the index finger of the string-hand being positioned to apply a locating pressure to the arrow. (ML)

Compared to a three-finger draw, the thumb occupies a smaller surface area of the string resulting in less friction and a faster, cleaner release; transferring more energy to the arrow. This is especially true when used with a solid thumb-ring. Here the string of even the heaviest bow sits on the tiniest ledge of a smooth, hard surface. Most importantly, the thumb-draw facilitates a faster loading speed. A right-handed archer wears his quiver on the right hip; from here an arrow can be drawn and placed on the right-hand side of the bow in the most ergonomic fashion. The thumb-draw also enabled a technique for rapid shooting that involved holding arrows in either the bow-hand or the string-hand.

The thumb-tab

It is apparent from art that the Egyptians, the Assyrians, the Hittites and others who used the angular bow did so by means of some style of thumb-release. To date no physical evidence of solid thumb-rings or shooting gloves has been discovered, but there is a clue that leather thumb-tabs may have been employed. That clue is what I consider to be a misidentified object in the collections of the Metropolitan Museum of Art, New York. Excavated at Thebes during 1926–27, it has been catalogued as an archer's wrist-guard and was found, still tied to the archer's wrist, in a mass grave of 59 soldiers. However, the dimensions – a fraction over 2 inches from top to bottom – suggest that it is absurdly small to be an effective wrist-guard. Both the shape and size are consistent with it being a thumb-guard.

The burial is dated to the reign of the Pharaoh Senwosret I (r. 1971–1926 BC), which is around 300 years prior to the arrival of the Hyksos. We may therefore deduce that the thumb-draw was in use in Egypt prior to the adoption of the composite bow. Moreover, it seems most probable that leather thumb-tabs remained in use into the age of the angular bow.

Replica of an Egyptian thumb-tab based on an example in the Metropolitan Museum of Art, New York. Made and tested by the author, it was found to work well. The curious little nipple at the apex of the tab was puzzling at first, but made sense in practical trials. It served as a locator between the base of the index and middle fingers, ensuring a consistent position and preventing the tab from slipping. (KH)

The bow-hand ring

An image (see page 57) of the Assyrian King Ashurbanipal, shooting from horseback, reveals a broad ring around the base of his bow-hand thumb. He is at full draw and presses his vertical thumb against the bow to hold the arrow securely prior to shooting, stabilizing it as he gallops and aims. The

narrowness of the angular bow enables this use of the bow-hand thumb. At the moment of shooting the thumb opens a fraction to allow unimpeded passage of the shaft. It is then that the thumb becomes the arrow-shelf, and this is where the ring comes into play.

In the Korean archery tradition it is common for a ring, made from a variety of materials, to be worn on the bow-hand thumb; it is known as the *san ji geun*, which translates as 'brace ring' (Koppedrayer 2002: 32). A bow-hand ring can occasionally be glimpsed in the art of other composite-bow cultures, and I suspect it was more widely used than representations would suggest.

The Sassanian shooting glove

An unusual form of lock appears in Sassanian art (AD 224–651), showing both the index finger and sometimes also the little finger extended. Only the back of the hand can be seen and the position of the thumb, middle and ring fingers is obscured. It is entirely possible that this draw was a two-finger draw, using only the middle and ring fingers. However, the slightly pronated wrist, evident in most of the art, is more consistent with it being a form of thumb-draw.

A bow-hand ring. With the thumb-draw, in which the arrow passes on the right-hand side of the bow, the base of the bow-hand thumb acts as an arrow-shelf. It is perfectly possible to shoot arrows over the bare hand, especially when the sharp quill ends are pared down and secured to the shaft by means of a silk binding, but the smooth shelf offered by a simple ring worn on the bow-hand thumb is an advantage, both for comfort and consistency. I use one made from leather and find it a boon – especially when using unbound, glued-on fletchings, which can otherwise lift and skewer the hand. (KH)

A possible interpretation of the construction and method of use for a Sassanian shooting glove, demonstrated by the author. The cross-strapping holds a thumb-tab securely in place. The tip of the thumb braces against the ring finger and is then locked by the middle finger. It is of note that in some styles of Japanese archery the index finger is extended along the shaft of the arrow in a similar manner. The purpose of extending the little finger is not clear and, in some depictions, it is folded. (KH)

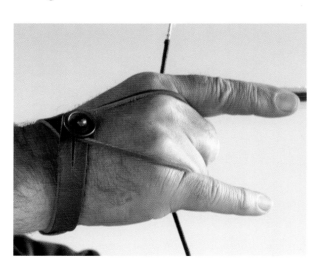

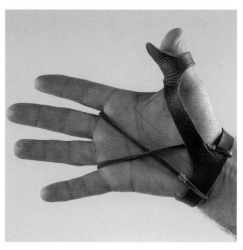

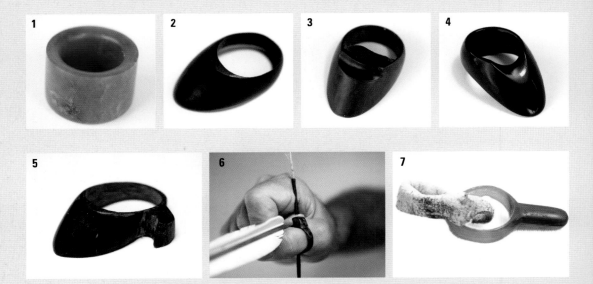

The solid thumb-ring

The ultimate, and most widely used, method for engaging the thumb-draw was with a solid thumb-ring. These provided, in effect, a trigger mechanism for the bow. Made of stone and cylindrical in form (**1**), the earliest archer's rings so far discovered have been excavated in north-eastern China and date to between 4700 BC and 2920 BC (Koppedrayer 2002: 19). Cylindrical rings are especially associated with China and Tibet, but they were not universal in all periods. Their most conspicuous ubiquity was during the Qing Dynasty (1644–1912) – the age of the Manchu and their mighty bows. I have a number, which I have picked up in street markets in China, and they feel strong and secure to shoot with. The cylindrical ring overlapped the crease of the joint, so that the thumb remained straighter than it did with a lipped ring. The thumb could still bend a little, owing to the concave bevel at the top of the ring, and this secured the ring from flying off. The lower portion of the ring, which had string contact, was convex. It was locked into place by the index finger at the tip of the thumb, rather than over it.

One advantage of the cylindrical ring for the military archer was that it always maintained the correct alignment, unlike the lipped ring. With the lipped ring there was the possibility, especially during intensive action, that it could rotate and misalign – a moment lost, a shot missed – before the archer could quickly twist it back into position.

The lipped ring consisted of a narrow band that sat just below the knuckle at the back of the hand and rose at an angle so that the ledge or groove of the ring was situated across the thumb crease on the inside of the hand. Extending from this little shelf was the lip, also known as the 'shield', which protected the thumb pad from the strike of the string on release.

On most lipped rings, it was the ledge at the base of the ring that retained the string (**2**); note how slim this ledge is and consider that the entire draw-weight of the bow is held by it. It offers an exceptionally clean and fast release. An alternative arrangement involved a groove near the base of the shield, to locate the string (**3**). Fit was critical – a ring that flew off the thumb in battle was both an inconvenience and an embarrassment. The oval aperture of the ring was placed onto the thumb with the shield to one side; it was then rotated so that the shield sat against the pad of the thumb. A properly fitted ring will stay in position and will neither rotate, nor slide down during use – such a ring is a prize beyond value and an archer will likely try many rings before he finds the right one. Several styles of Chinese lipped rings, especially from the Ming Dynasty, had a V-shaped notch at the base to accommodate the protuberance of flesh created when the thumb bends; a replica is shown here (**4**).

Another variant of the thumb-ring, common in China during the Warring States period (475–221 BC) but also noted occasionally on Turkish rings, was the spur ring (**5**), a lipped ring with a curved projection to one side. In use, the curve of this spur cradled the shaft immediately in front of the nock, and, with a bulbous nock, acted to hold the arrow in place by pushing it back against the string in the line of draw (**6**). This contrasted with the usual manner of holding the arrow in place securely, which was by means of lateral pressure from the index finger. It is an easy fault to exert too much pressure, thus distorting the lie of the string, and it may be to address this problem that the spur ring was developed. It offered an opposing lateral pressure to counter that of the index finger. Relying primarily on backward pressure and neutralizing any lateral pressure would have been especially advantageous when using arrows with shallow nocks – such arrows were commonplace.

8

9

10

11

Surprisingly, despite their evident ingenuity, spur rings never achieved widespread use.

In Korean archery there were two distinct styles of thumb-ring. The *sugakji* (**7**), known as the male ring, was not really a thumb-ring at all in the conventional sense, but rather a release-aid that was worn on the thumb. The thumb inserted into the ring and the prong, secured by the index finger, hooked over the string. It acted as a latch to hold, draw and release. The *amgakji* (**8**), known as the female ring, was similar to other lipped rings from elsewhere, though the shield tended to be longer on Korean rings; a replica in the author's collection is shown here.

Thumb-rings were made from various materials including horn, bone, ivory, antler, hardwoods, several types of stone – especially jade – and metals including iron, bronze, brass or silver. There is considerable variation in the size of rings and some materials tend to be bulkier than others. Everyone had their preferences, but silver rings (**9**) – a replica in the author's collection is shown here – enjoyed particular favour. A metal ring can be made with finer proportions and yet still be mechanically strong. For use on horseback, where the ability to reload rapidly was a key component, a smaller, daintier ring interfered much less with the nimble dexterity of the thumb, index finger and middle finger – the active digits for speed-nocking techniques.

Some, but not all, rings employed a thin leather insert, called a *kulak* (**3** and **9**). This both refined the fit and created greater friction against the thumb to thwart rotation or slipping in the heat of action. The lower portion of the *kulak*, a tiny tab known as the *kash*, extends beyond the ledge. It provides a flat surface behind the string so that any bulges of flesh, created by flexing the thumb, do not get pinched between the string and the ledge of the ring.

Archer's rings became high-status ornaments, attesting not only to the wearer's good taste and wealth, but also to his warrior standing. Indian portraiture of maharajas and other high-ranking

nobility, both Hindu and Muslim, frequently shows that the ring has been reversed when worn in a non-military context – the shield sits on the back of the thumb. It has been suggested (Koppedrayer 2002: 32) that this was a symbol of peaceful intent – that the wearer simultaneously proclaimed his prowess as an archer, while indicating that he was not about to shoot anyone at that moment.

The materials from which thumb-rings were made invited elaborate decoration. A Persian thumb-ring made of white jade with a floral design created by an inlay of pink and green tourmaline and gold outline is shown here (**10**); it dates from between the 17th and 19th centuries. Thumb-rings could be carved, incised, inset with gold or silver wire and embedded with fine jewels. On occasion a ring might become so embellished with surface adornment that it was no longer suitable for its intended purpose. Such rings were worn at court solely as jewellery. A particular feature of Qing Dynasty rings is that they were usually carried in exquisitely ornate cases, made from appliquéd silk, intricately carved wood, ivory or jade, and during the Zhou Dynasty there were protocols at formal gatherings that ritualized the putting on of the thumb-ring (Koppedrayer 2002: 26).

Even after the introduction of other materials to make solid thumb-rings, leather remained in widespread use for defending the thumb (**11**). The author of *Arab Archery* is a proponent of the virtues of leather thumb-rings, considering that they offer sensitivity similar to shooting with a bare thumb. He advises that they be made with medium-thickness leather and lined with fine leather, adding that they should be indented with a groove for the string (Faris & Elmer 1945: 123). I shot with a leather ring for some time before acting on the advice to incise a groove for the string. I found it immensely useful to be able quickly to feel a correct and consistent alignment for the string. (All photos courtesy KH except **7** and **10**, courtesy UM)

Thumb-ring techniques

Shooting with the thumb-draw is an arcane art and when used with a solid thumb-ring, the technique becomes even more nuanced. It is significantly more difficult to learn than the three-finger draw and beginners all too frequently quit early on, finding it too difficult. Shooting the composite bow in an authentic manner is a sophisticated martial art. A solid thumb-ring creates the archery equivalent of the hair-trigger. The entire weight of the draw is held on an extremely narrow surface, and the slightest inconsistency in angles and alignments can cause the string to slip from the ring prematurely. It is a wonderful teacher and yet also an unforgiving taskmaster; errors frequently cause pain to either thumb or index finger. With each increase in draw-weight there is less tolerance for error and the reproving lash of the string becomes even harsher. Eventually, consistency is drilled into the archer's form and the reward of a fast, clean release is immense.

Closely allied to the draw with the thumb-ring is the push with the bow-hand and consequent follow-through, known as the *khatrah*. Taybughā teaches: 'What the archer should do is to dip the bow sharply from the grip in such a way that at the moment the string is loosed he would appear to give his arrow a push with the string. The action must be strongly executed and come from the wrist-joint like the punch of a man in anger' (quoted in Latham & Paterson 1970: 68).

In numerous manuscript images, archers who have just shot display this characteristic forward-cocked wrist. Taybughā counsels that it is a great fault to anticipate the action, which would result in a dropped bow-arm, and equally poor form to mimic it after the event. It should be the outcome of correct shooting style, emphasizing the push with the left arm in equal measure to the pull with the right. According to Taybughā, 'the movement increases both cast and range' (quoted in Latham & Paterson 1970: 68).

Similar follow-throughs are advocated by various old masters, including that of allowing the bow to spin a half-rotation to the left on release – a technique still greatly valued by Japanese *kyudo* archers. The essence is that these movements of the bow should be a natural consequence of a clean release, not something to fake for display.

The Chinese general and writer on military matters Tang Jingchuan (1507–60) recommended a similar procedure but with a lot of unnecessary flourish, suggesting the 'bow tip painted the ground' and the 'draw hand snapped back with the palm upturned slightly' (quoted in Tian & Ma 2015: 140). Such affectation was roundly condemned by Gao Ying some decades later. He scoffed that 'Youngsters love this flowery style of release, but they fail to recognize its faults' (quoted in Tian & Ma 2015: 140).

As the composite bow developed and diversified, so too did schools of thought for optimal shooting styles. The steady shot of the long-range sniper, target-shooter or hunter required nuances in technique that differed from the demands of the horse-archer, galloping at high speed and with only seconds to let fly as many arrows as possible while operating at an effective range. For him, the snap and push of the *khatrah* aided both his performance and his instinctive aiming ability. To my mind a properly executed *khatrah* is an exciting, decisive, attacking style of shooting that only adds to the thrill of using this powerful weapon.

USE
Archery – a very martial art

THE CHARIOT-ARCHER

During the Zhou Dynasty (*c.*1046–256 BC) the Chinese used chariot archery extensively. However, for the purposes of this discussion, I confine my observations to the early chariot cultures of the Near East and their use of the angular bow.

Angular bows were employed by infantry archers, horse-archers and chariot-archers, but it was as the weapon of the chariot-archer that this early form of the composite bow made its most dramatic and consequential entry onto the battlefields of antiquity. It was a principal weapon of

In battle, a driver accompanied the chariot-archer. I have driven chariots on the plains of Troy (Hisarlik) and the sands of Giza and common to both these arid landscapes were the clouds of dust generated by pounding hooves and spinning wheels. Chariots creaked and rattled onto ancient battlefields by the several thousand. Such squalling squadrons would have whipped up dust storms of great magnitude – in places reducing visibility to a few feet. Here, the author is the archer in a replica Egyptian chariot (built by Robert Hurford) carrying a replica angular bow (built by Lukas Novotny). The bow remains outside the perimeter of the confined space of the chariot body at all times. I have shot an angular bow from a number of Egyptian, Hittite and Assyrian chariot replicas; the space is very tight indeed. Quivers were mounted externally to the vehicle and placed with ergonomic convenience for the archer. With this arrangement the arrow pulls into place on the right-hand side of the bow; the correct side for shooting an arrow by means of a thumb-draw. (Photograph by Robert Hurford)

Egyptians, Hittites, Assyrians and other military cultures of the Ancient Near East. Compared to wooden bows, the shorter limb length of the angular bow offered a distinct advantage when managing a bow in the cramped space of the chariot platform. The archer stood next to a driver and needed to be able to shoot in all directions.

For exhibition shooting, however, it was usual for the archer to ride solo with the reins tied around his waist. There is an account of the Pharaoh Amenhotep II (r. 1427–1401 BC) shooting arrows at a copper ingot target from his galloping chariot:

Detail of the platform on a replica Egyptian chariot (built by Robert Hurford). Widths for Egyptian chariots varied between 36 inches and 43 inches. From front to back, the woven-rawhide, sprung platform was around 20 inches or less. In order to stabilize, when shooting forwards or to the side from a jolting vehicle at high speed, it helps to brace the right foot on the bar that forms the rear of the platform frame and lean the left hip into the front rail. When shooting to the rear, the archer simply turns and leans against the side. The narrow depth of these platforms enables these braced positions without compromising a vertical stance. (ML)

he entered into his northern garden and found that there had been set up for him four targets of Asiatic copper of one palm in their thickness, with 20 cubits between one post and its fellow. Then His Majesty appeared in a chariot like Montu [the Egyptian god of war] in his power. He grasped his bow and gripped four arrows at the same time. So he rode northward, shooting at them ... (Pritchard 1969: 244)

Chariot battle between Egyptians and Hittites (opposite)

A pall of thick dust generated by the stampede of horses and the spin of wheels has created very limited visibility. Chariot-to-chariot warfare may be analogous to the aerial dogfights of World War II, with an enemy suddenly appearing out of the clouds, and it was the job of the driver to position the archer for maximum advantage. We may imagine a constant swirling, skidding and jockeying for position as drivers manoeuvred their teams not only defensively but also to avail the archer of his best shot. Engagement in the optimal position may only last for a few seconds and the ability to shoot rapidly was of great advantage.

Although it is entirely possible to shoot from either side of the chariot – switching places with the driver is an easy two-step dance – images in art and the configuration of quivers on surviving Egyptian chariots suggest that the archer stood predominantly to the left of the driver. This contrasts with Chinese chariot-archers, who stood to the right of the driver (Selby 2000: 144). The latter positioning seems more expedient because the resulting angles between driver and archer would allow the archer to come to full draw without risk of knocking the driver with his elbow.

Horses must surely have been primary targets in such encounters, but light, flexible scale armour, constructed from pieces of hardened rawhide sewn to a multilayered fabric base, offered reasonable protection to large areas. Similar armour, with either leather or bronze scales, was worn to defend the torsos of the archers and drivers who could afford it. Thick leather sidings to the chariot body offered the occupants a good defence from the waist down.

Even when his vehicle was immobilized, the chariot-archer, provided that he remained relatively unscathed, could still undertake a useful role in the battle by sniping from behind the wreckage.

This reference to grasping four arrows at the same time suggests the early use of speed-shooting techniques with the composite bow; arrows held in the bow-hand ready to be nocked in rapid succession. A cubit is reckoned to be around 20 inches (less by some calculations), which means that Amenhotep's targets were approximately 11 yards apart. If we assume, as surely we must, that he was galloping his chariot, then this represented a very impressive rate of shooting. Equally impressive was the power of the shots. Copper ingots used as targets were traditionally in the shape of hides. These were standard trade commodities, harking back to a time when animal hides had been trading currency. The regular size was probably an inch or less thick and the 'one palm' thickness suggests that Amenhotep's targets may have consisted of multiple copper sheets placed back to back.

Such shooting displays, with the reins tied around the waist, were customary demonstrations for pharaohs affirming their martial prowess. I have tried this and found that, for the forward shot, it was possible to adjust and maintain the direction of the horses by slight movements of the torso. However to turn and shoot to the side or to the rear required twisting at the waist to an extent that caused the horses to veer. With targets set up at an approximately 45-degree angle to a straight track, the forward shot was achievable – it being a slight diagonal from the line of travel, rather than directly over the horses' heads.

In battle, each chariot had its *peherer* (runner), armed with a spear. His duties might range from adjusting harness, changing over a horse team or clearing obstacles to replenishing arrow supplies, marshalling captives or repelling boarders in a skirmish. The stamina and swiftness of today's long-distance runners is evidence enough that it would be possible for elite men to maintain contact with the vehicle in most circumstances. At times they might also ride on the chariot and act as a shield-bearer, but such discussions threaten to divert from the main theme. There can be little doubt, though, that the *peherer* would have been of considerable support, and in defensive positions these spearmen might deploy with the archers to form a protective hedge.

When going up against formed infantry a chariot would be too vulnerable if it ran parallel to the front line, even with armoured horses. In my view it would have been more likely that chariots attacked, in troops of ten, in a wheeling charge. I envisage parallel troops attacking at a slight angle towards the enemy front line to give the archers a clear shot without shooting directly over the team ahead. When they neared the enemy line they would turn sharply, minimizing the time they presented their vulnerable flanks, and continue in a loop. It may be no coincidence that this configuration corresponds to the elongated oval of a Roman chariot-racing circuit; echoes of the ancient chariot attack pattern? The archer would have been able to shoot continuously on both the approach and the withdrawal and to repeat this manoeuvre over and over again. *Peherers* stationed at the home end of the circuit would have been able to re-supply with armfuls of arrows. They would also have had no more than a 200-yard dash to run in with a replacement horse team.

Certainly these tactics of attack and retreat are those identified as the tactics of the chariot-archer's successor – the horse-archer.

THE HORSE-ARCHER: ORIGINS

It was the Assyrians who transferred the skills of the chariot-archer to those of the horse-archer in combat. At some point around the 9th century BC they deployed horse-archers, shooting angular bows, in battle. Curiously, Assyrian reliefs of the time show pairs of riders, one an archer and the other a horseman alongside, holding the reins of the archer's horse. It evokes the companion bond that must have been established between a chariot-driver and his archer. Both are riding bareback with just a saddle-cloth. I have done this, in a pot-holed, rock-strewn gully in Turkey, with a companion riding alongside and taking the reins of my horse. Surrendering control of one's horse in this way is deeply unnerving, and although I managed to shoot and hit the target, I could perceive no benefit to having a co-rider. Soon enough such an idea was abandoned and the horse-archer proper thundered onto the ancient battlefield.

It is possible that nomadic steppe peoples developed the idea of shooting their bows from horseback even earlier than this, and that these two strands of development were independent, but archaeology has yet to yield a definitive verdict. Either way, the composite bow in the hands of the horse-archer created a new breed of warrior – one who was to dominate the battlefields of the Eastern World for many centuries to come. The power of the composite bow combined with the speed and mobility of the horse created a new force in warfare – one that had the ability to establish empires.

A modern drawing of a detail from the north wall at Abu Simbel. It is the earliest known depiction (to date) of an archer on horseback. Dating to around 1264 BC, this image existed several hundred years before the emergence of horse-archers as a force on the battlefield. Armed with an angular composite bow, the rider is probably a messenger; it is difficult to know if he carries the bow for dismounted defence, or whether it was shot from horseback. Note his position, the so-called 'donkey seat'. Riding bareback, he is perched on the hindquarters of the horse. Representations in art of the earliest riders invariably depict them in this manner, possibly because horses had not yet been bred with sufficient bone and muscle to carry a man in a more forward position. It is a less secure position from which to ride and shoot. (Illustration by David Joseph Wright)

Saddles, stirrups and the rise of the horse-archer

It is perfectly possible to shoot a bow from a horse while riding bareback. I do so at the gallop as part of my regular practice, and many Native American tribes – most notably the Comanche – were accustomed to shooting bareback both for war and hunting, although by the 19th century they also used various forms of saddle-pad and saddle.

There have been many horse-archer cultures – among them Assyrians, Scythians and Parthians – who shot their bows from horseback using either saddle-pads or saddles without the additional aid of stirrups. A saddle and stirrups, or lack of, is not a determining factor to being able to shoot a bow from horseback. That is not to say that a saddle does not make a difference; it does. It helps with stability and, more importantly, it is the rigid saddletree that allows for the suspension of stirrups. Stirrups are a considerable aid to the archer, making it possible for him to change his posture on the horse. With stirrups he can stand slightly and lean a little forward, enlisting his knees to be the fulcrum of suspension, while still supporting some of his weight on his feet. He rises to separate himself from the motions of the horse in order to achieve a smoother shot.

Although various proto-stirrup systems, such as toe loops and a single stirrup to aid mounting, pre-date the development of paired stirrups, it was this latter that was of significance to the archer. The breakthrough was made, during the latter part of the 5th century AD, by the Xiongnu, a people originating to the west of China and generally thought to have been the antecedents of the Huns – they were a horse-archer people.

I would further suggest that a major advantage of stirrups is that they facilitate the use of heavier bows from horseback. For any man's given strength, he is able to shoot a heavier bow from the ground than he is from horseback. A strong man can shoot a much heavier bow from horseback than can a weakling from the ground, of course, and because of such individual variation it is impossible to ascribe precise values to a comparison. Nevertheless, there remains a general principle that the infantry archer is able to draw a heavier bow than the mounted man because he employs his whole body to do so.

The characteristic stance of the heavy bow shooter, whether he be an English longbowman or a Manchu archer with his great composite bow, is with flexed knees and an angled torso that tilts the pelvis, in the manner of a weightlifter, to both protect the spine from vertebral compression and to recruit all the muscles, including those of the legs, into the power of the draw. Conversely, a man sitting on a horse with his seat in contact with the saddle has to rely on his upper body strength alone. Now mighty men have great upper-body strength and undoubtedly strong bows were in use on horseback before the stirrup appeared, but the archer's strength was not fully optimized when seated, thus limiting his full potential.

Few people today shoot bows of a realistic military weight and so this image of the archer with his tilted pelvis, though common in art, often seems strange to modern eyes, more used to observing recreational archers shooting bows of modest weights (below 70lb). It was nevertheless, historically, the stance of the power shooter. By rising in the stirrups and angling forward, the horse-archer mimicked closely the posture of the infantry archer drawing a heavy bow. There was some slight loss of power because an amount was diverted into maintaining balance on the moving horse, but stirrups enabled the archer to harness significantly more of his total body strength into the draw than would have been possible otherwise. For example – the following figures are notional and the ratios speculative – a man who can draw a 100lb bow on the ground may well be able to draw an 80lb bow on horseback with stirrups, but may only manage a 60lb bow without stirrups.

There were other benefits to stirrups – such as ease in mounting taller horses, lessening the fatigue of long-distance riding, enabling a ridden horse to jump higher obstacles, and aiding stability for impact combat (a job done fairly well previously by the four-horned saddle) – but by far the greatest contribution of the stirrup was as an aid to the horse-archer.

THE HORSE-ARCHER PREPARES FOR WAR

The art and literature of the composite bow gives scant information on the precise use of this weapon in war, but it is rich with examples of how it was used for courtly entertainment, as public display and in competition and training. It is from these glimpses of what was possible, what was done, that we must extrapolate its deployment on the battlefield.

Horses and the horse-archer

There were two distinct types of horse that gave rise to different horse-archer traditions – the steppe pony and the Turkoman/Arab horse.

From the broad swathe of grassland plains – the steppe – which stretched, broken only by the Altai Mountains, across Eurasia from China, through Mongolia, Kazakhstan and the Ukraine to its outposts on the Pannonian Plain of Hungary, came the steppe pony. These large-headed, squat, shaggy horses carried the Mongol Horde to create the largest contiguous Empire the world has ever seen, and Attila and his Huns rode into Europe on steeds of a similar stamp.

Men would travel with a string of horses, sleeping in the saddle. Additional horses simply ran with the herd. The Archdeacon Thomas of Split (13th century), describing the Mongol host, wrote, 'However many horses a man possesses, they are so trained that they follow him like dogs' (quoted in Jankovich 1971: 65). Riders would switch horses to spare the animals fatigue but they remained mounted constantly. It meant that an army on the move never had to stop. *The Secret History of the Mongols*, written anonymously a few years after the death of Genghis Khan in 1227, cites one of his orders regarding the treatment of horses on the march: 'Bridles will not be worn on the march – the horses are to have their mouths free' (quoted in Jankovich 1971: 64). These hardy little horses could sustain themselves from the rough grazing they found on the way. There was no need for wagons to carry supplies of oats, hay and other fodder, as required for other types of military mount. No farriers were needed for their tough unshod hooves. Such lumbering logistics did not slow the inexorable advance of a nomad army.

Furthermore, these horses were naturally inclined to the fifth gait – a type of very fast walk known as the amble. It is a motion in which both legs on one side moved forward together in a single stride, sequenced by both legs on the other side. It provided an exceptionally smooth ride that was less tiring for the rider. Moreover it was a gait that the horse could sustain for many miles, hour after hour, maintaining speeds between 10 and 15 miles per hour.

Steppe ponies were equally capable of galloping for short bursts in a battle but it was their ability to keep going, without pause, day after day, which earned a reputation for surprise attack. A Mongol army that was estimated, by scouts, to be days away, might suddenly arrive the following dawn. In action these little horses were effective, but they lacked the élan and excitement of horses from the desert.

In complete contrast, the hard-rock deserts of Turkmenistan and Kazakhstan, in the foothills of the Altai, gave rise to the Turkoman horse – a fiery whirlwind of equine fury, a smooth-coated, hot-blooded animal with a warrior's heart. This area was the homeland of the Oghuz and other Turkish tribes before they migrated to create the Seljuq Empire in the 11th century. They brought these courageous horses with them. Today the breed is considered extinct, though it lives on in the form of the Akhal-Teké, an equally tough, fast and spirited horse of immense stamina. These horses were high-maintenance beasts, however, often fed on diets that might include mutton fat, chicken, barley, raisins and dates – a quartermaster's nightmare.

From the sands of Arabia emerged the spirited, snorting hauteur of the Arab horse, with its fine bones, characteristic small head and dished face; it too was a sleek and slender speed machine. Alike in both appearance and temperament to the Turkoman, the Arab horse also required considerably more care and logistic support and was fed on a similar diet.

In combat both the Arab and the Turkoman possessed unequalled boldness, dash and pace. Companies of horse-archers could appear from nowhere in an instant, strike, disappear and reappear, and they could outpace anyone reckless enough to attempt pursuit. They were the ultimate masters of hit-and-run tactics on the battlefield, of encirclement and the scourge of the marching column.

The more slender build of these desert breeds was conducive to greater flexibility in the saddle for the horse-archer, who could turn and angle his shots forwards, back, up, down and to the opposite side of the horse's neck with greater ease and agility. These majestic horses brought excitement, verve and flair to the business of the horse-archer and he cultivated it into an art.

The author demonstrating the forward shot from horseback. A horse-archer rises to shoot. In this way he achieves relative stillness and minimizes the vibrations and bounce from the horse's movement that might affect the shot; his knees acting as a suspension system. In this position he also assumes a semi-standing posture, with a tilted pelvis, that is broadly similar to the stance of an infantry archer shooting a heavy draw-weight bow. Not only is the spine protected from compression injury, but the archer is also able to engage the muscles of his core and his legs into supporting the draw; conversely, the seated man can only draw with his arms. (KH)

The *qabaq*

Arguably the most spectacular and demanding skill for the horse-archer was to shoot at the *qabaq*. *Qabaq* means 'gourd', and gourd-shooting was an extremely popular form of training, competition and exhibition for horse-archers throughout the Middle East and Persia.

Actual gourds were the most common form of target, though for higher-status events these were substituted with an artificial gourd constructed from a precious metal such as gold or silver; it remained possible to penetrate it with an arrow. In the modern incarnation of *qabaq*, a metal plate is used and shot at with blunt arrows, hits being registered acoustically.

Another variation was to have birds in a cage atop the pole. The objective was not to shoot the birds themselves, but rather to release them by the arrow striking some form of latch. A more challenging alternative was to have birds tethered to the mast by cords. In order to set them free the archer had to cut the cords with a crescent-headed arrow. This was theatre.

It is an old confusion to think that shooting at aerial targets on masts is practice for shooting birds. More probably, *qabaq* originated as a practice for horse-archers riding the perimeter of fortified towns or castles and shooting up at defenders. Such actions are portrayed in art. Nevertheless, it was as a means of displaying martial prowess that shooting at the *qabaq* found most favour.

Taybughā sounded a word of caution to the gourd-shooter, whose gaze was perforce focused on his elevated target, saying that he 'should beware of his horse bumping into the mast and ... keep a man's arm's length between his horse and the mast' (quoted in Latham & Paterson 1970: 76). Such a narrow margin exacted both highly skilled horsemanship and shooting: the shorter the distance between rider and mast, the more the shot was admired. The risks of such a tactic were evident from the fact that Taybughā also reported that His Excellency Azdamur, the Viceroy of Tripoli (in Syria), riding before a crowd of applauding onlookers, took his attention away from his horse, with the consequence that they collided with the mast. Both the Viceroy and his horse were killed (Latham & Paterson 1970: 76).

Perhaps with this incident in mind, Taybughā offered an alternative method of practice for this feat, which was to

This copy of a detail from a manuscript miniature (Hazine 1523 f138a) in Istanbul's Topkapi Palace Museum depicts Sultan Murad II (r. 1421–44 and 1446–51) shooting the *qabaq*. In this exercise a gourd was placed on top of a mast approximately 25 feet tall and archers, riding by at a fierce gallop, endeavoured to pierce it with their arrows. It was a thrilling exercise, with the archer often positioned at extreme angles alongside the horse's neck in order to achieve a direct line of vertical shot parallel to the pole. Hits could be achieved at shallower angles, either approaching or going away from the target, but it was the true vertical shot that won the most acclaim. (Illustration by David Joseph Wright)

mark a circle on the ground. The idea was that if the archer shot sufficiently vertically as he passed the mark, the arrow would land in the circle, by which time one's horse would have sped its rider to a safe distance – not an exercise to be attempted with a horse that is not sufficiently forward-going!

The *furūsiyya* track

A rare example of target arrangements for the practice of horse-archery is contained in a 14th-century military manual, *Münyetü'l-Ġuzāt* (*Wish of the Warriors of the Faith*), which describes the stages of progression that a horse-archer should undergo:

> When you wish to start shooting arrows on horseback while riding, you should take a weak bow and arrow(s) which are good for this skill. Then erect five barcas [targets] that are following each other. The distance between each of them should be forty arshins. Then take five arrows, ride your horse fast and shoot these one after the other. When you become good at shooting at these, make the distance between them thirty arshins. Every time reduce (the distance between the barcas) like that, until the distance is seven steps. (Öztopçu 1986: 199)

An *arshin* equates to around 28 inches, so 40 *arshins* equals approximately 31 yards. That is the approximate distance between targets for some modern horse-archery courses. I can hit all the targets with that distance between them, even on a very fast horse. Reducing that distance incrementally is one thing, but taking it down to seven steps between targets defies the imagination. The author goes on to humble us further:

> When you also become skillful at this, try to shoot fast. This [seven-step distance] is the limit in this practice. Then erect them in another way, that is to say, three barcas on your left side and opposite to them two barcas on your right side. Then ride fast, come and shoot first at the ones that are on your left side and then at the ones that are on your right, if you can. When you become skillful also at this, take a strong bow and shoot with it in the same way that you had done with a weak bow. Once you have perfected your accurate shooting, from then on you will shoot accurately everywhere, that is to say, in the time of war, while shooting deer and in the hippodromes. From then on you will not be afraid of shooting arrows. (Öztopçu 1986: 199)

Not only does the master require faster shooting and quicker riding, he demands the ability to shoot on either side of the horse. Then, lest the student should become conceited with his abilities, he is told to discard the weak 'starter' bow he was advised to begin with and take up a bow with a heavy draw-weight. Draw-weight makes an immense difference to the ability to shoot rapidly. It is comparatively easy to do so with a lightweight bow, but shooting at speed necessitates not only a fast nocking technique but also the ability to pull the string back to full draw very quickly – there is no time for a gradual draw. To do so without injury calls for both flawless technique and immense strength and anything less than full draw diminishes the military effectiveness of the shot. In the final passage of this section, the bar is raised even higher:

> Then erect ten barcas, five of them on your left and five of them on your right in various places. The distance between each of them should be in accordance with the limit that we had mentioned earlier. Take ten arrows that are suitable for this practice. Hold five of them together with the grip (of the bow) and insert (the other) five between the fingers of your right hand. When you finish shooting the arrows that were between your fingers, take the arrows next to the grip and insert them between your fingers, then shoot them as before. These arrows should be thin, so that they will fit between your fingers while you shoot. (Öztopçu 1986: 200)

Here he is advocating a larger than usual in-hand arsenal by employing both the bow-hand and the draw-hand to hold arrows. To be able to shoot this fast, with a heavy bow, and at targets on either side is simply astonishing.

Training for horse-archery (opposite)

Here, an Ottoman horse-archer trains according to a system set out in a 14th-century *furūsiyya* manual – *Münyetü' l-Ġuzāt* – now in the Topkapi Sarayi Müzesi, Istanbul. He has an arrow on the string and is at full draw. Two arrows have been shot and he retains a further two in his draw-hand. An additional five arrows are held in the bow-hand, making ten in all for the prescribed course. The targets, constructed from sand-filled wicker baskets with a cloth facing, have been placed both to the left and the right of the track. The distance between each target has been reduced from the 31 yards suggested for beginners to a barely believable 'seven steps', which the manual requires for the best archers.

The text specifies the arrangement for carrying arrows in each hand, and recommends that they are thin. It is plain that the more slender the arrowshaft, the greater the number that can be comfortably held in the hand, and such speed-shooting techniques are limited to lighter arrows. However, it is probable that arrow-carriage with this number of in-hand arrows was reserved for the display ground and the competition track. It was less suitable for the battlefield.

For a right-handed archer, shooting at the targets on the right-hand side is especially challenging. He has the option to switch the bow to his right hand but must otherwise take the bow over the horse's neck. A shorter bow is an advantage in doing this. Simply twisting at the waist is not enough to set up for the shot. The elbow of the string-hand needs to be aligned with the bow-arm and for this to happen in the saddle, the archer must rise and pivot and also adjust the position of his legs, requiring an athletic agility.

Under Ottoman rule large areas, specifically for archery, were established in many cities. Known as *ok meydani* (arrow places), these massive arenas were for training, for competition and for lavish public display. The *ok meidan* was where infantry archers would hold contests in flight-shooting and target-shooting, as well as being a place for the horse-archer to practise and perform. Together with their trainers and staff the top archers – professional athletes and martial artists – were accommodated within the purlieu of the grounds. Archery was held in very high regard and the best archers enjoyed considerable celebrity.

The Ottoman track

A 17th-century Ottoman manual of military horsemanship, the *Kitab-ı Makbûl der-Hâl-i Huyûl*, describes elaborate mounted exercises that incorporated the use of the bow together with the sword, the mace and the shield; giving us insight into the dynamic, multi-weapon virtuosity of the horse-archer and his capabilities on the battlefield. My thanks to Gökmen Altınkulp for information on this manuscript, which is not currently available in English translation.

All the drills required the archer to be ambidextrous, making alternate runs of the track shooting to the right with the bow in the right hand and then shooting to the left with the bow in the left hand; for some of the more advanced exercises, the bow had to be switched mid-course. The archer was also required to maintain constant contact with the reins by means of a small finger loop attached to the reins by a lanyard, which he held in his bow-hand.

Of particular note was the deployment of the *kalkan* (shield) while shooting. Suspended by a strap, the shield had to be shifted nimbly from shoulder to shoulder according to which hand held the bow. For a right-handed-shot (bow in left hand) to a target on the left, the shield had to be on the right shoulder, and vice versa. There was much emphasis placed on the ability to swiftly switch bow and *kalkan* between runs.

Nearly 20 different drills are described, ranging from simple three-shot runs, drawing arrows from the quiver, to courses that demanded an arrow be shot both going towards and going away from each target. For this doubling attack, hitting each target with a one–two shot, it was recommended that additional arrows were carried in the string-hand.

More complex exercises required a combination of archery and strikes with the sword. In one example the archer is instructed to unsheath the sword, hang it from the right arm, take three arrows, nock one and put the other two between the fingers of the string-hand. *At the gallop*, he is then required to shoot forwards into the first target; then shoot behind himself to the same target; shoot the third arrow at the *qabaq* target; cut at the next sword target, sheath the sword; then shoot at the next target. For another run, which focused on the low sand-mound targets, the archer was not permitted to nock the arrow until after he had passed the target. Some courses required all three sword targets to be struck in addition to archery shots. Likewise, the mace was incorporated to attack the sword targets. One run required setting the mace on the first sand-pile, shooting the bow on approach, picking up the mace, twirling it three times, striking a target with it, then shooting at the *qabaq*, then drawing the sword and cutting a target to the right.

Even more extreme feats were summoned for archers who could shoot at a target on the approach, then – while still at full gallop – unstring and restring their bow, cut at a sword target, followed by a shot at the *qabaq* and finally slice a gourd in two with their sword. By comparison, leaning out of the saddle at the gallop to collect one's arrows from a sand-pile at the start of the run (another recommended exercise), was relatively elementary.

The constant switching from sword to bow to mace and the swapping of the shield from one shoulder to the other demonstrated tremendous versatility

A court spectacle

On 21 July 1582, Queen Elizabeth I's ambassador to the Ottoman court, William Harborne, witnessed an elaborate military tattoo in Constantinople. According to his account of the event, 100 horsemen gave a demonstration of martial skills, which included *qabaq* shooting and other feats with the bow:

A very long mast with a golden ball at the top of it was planted in the middle of the Hippodrome, and on one side and the other in a straight line were planted two rows of trenchers [wooden plates] with a little blank in the middle, on rods six quarte high from the ground, and over against them was extended on the ground a log of wood representing a man. These marks were laid in order a good hand-cast apart.

The horseman rode straight for them, and at the beginning of the course drew his sword, aimed a blow at the log, at once replaced his sword, shot an arrow at the ball on the mast, and at once taking another from his quiver shot it at the other mark, almost as the course was ending. This was done by all, always in one course.

Then they ran with their arrows only, shooting the first at the first mark, and taking another smartly shot at the mast, and then did the same at the last mark, always at full speed, and returned to do the same feats with the left hand.

Then some ran with shields, shooting the arrow with the right hand and holding the shield in the left, and then put the shield in the right and shot with the left, doing all this at unbroken speed.

Others, with sword and arrow, shifting the sword to the right hand and the left, did marvellous things.

Others after shooting their arrows, drew their swords, and rising from their horses touched the ground with one foot, struck a blow and remounted instantly with much dexterity, aimed a second arrow at the mark at the end of their course, doing it to right and left alike; and certainly very few shots went astray, some having in one course hit all the marks except the ball ...

Very good were those shots when riding one after another they turned, looking backwards, and shot the arrow behind them, hitting the mark to the great marvel of everyone. (CSPF 1909: 170–88)

Harborne was at pains to point out that everything was done 'at full speed' and his report went on to describe equestrian acrobatics and the throwing of javelins. What marvellous theatre it must have been, and a drama that emphasized not only the archery skills of the horse-archer but also his proficiency with other weapons. Ability with the bow was the most esteemed, but expertise with the shield and the sword carried almost equal regard.

Javelins, usually in a case of three, were commonly carried by Turkish, Persian and Mamluk horse-archers as additional missiles and, although not a feature of the display that Harborne witnessed, aptitude with the lance was almost always a part of the horse-archer's martial repertoire. Whether Hunnic, Mongol, Tatar or Chinese, whether Mamluk *fāris*, Persian or Turkish, almost all horse-archers also carried the lasso as a battlefield weapon – with echoes of their nomadic herding origin. Not only was it used to haul a man from his horse; it was a primary tool for the taking of prisoners. The horse-archer was an extremely versatile warrior, one for whom training was a daily exercise.

When the Turkish bow was in use, the grip, which was often highly decorated, was covered with a wrap of waxed linen called a *mushamma*. This narrow bandage, wound on spirally, also enabled the size and shape of the grip to be customized precisely to the archer's hand. An alternative to the traditional *mushamma* was to bind the grip with a strip of leather, protecting the grip against tarnish from the hand and abrasion from the arrow. (KH)

A view of a replica *hilal kuram* bow built by Lukas Novotny, showing the *bash*, which is the non-bending 'lever' at the tip of the bow. Note that the sinew layers on the back of the bow are covered with leather and the horn on the belly of the bow is polished and left uncovered. Both are decorated with gold paint. (KH)

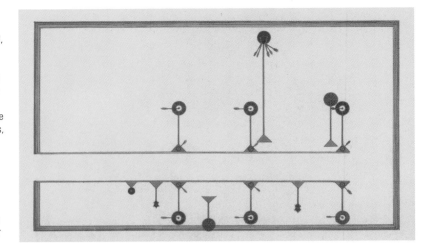

A modern copy of the track plan illustrated in the *Kitab-ı Makbûl der-Hâl-i Huyûl*. It depicts a broad, straight track, around 8 yards wide and 190 yards in length. In the original manuscript distances are given in bow-lengths (a bow-length approximates to 3 feet 5 inches). To the left of the track are three archery targets set on posts, roughly 60 yards apart. These also have secondary targets, in the form of rope circlets placed on sand mounds, at the foot of the posts. Additionally to the left, there is a *qabaq* target. The penultimate target on this side is a post-mounted target set further back from the track. To the right of the track, for left-handed shots, are also three archery targets on posts with secondary targets on sand mounds at their bases. A fourth post-mounted target is set back further from the track between the first and second archery targets. Also to the right of the track are three targets (possibly gourds) for either the sword or the mace. One is placed on a knee-high mound of sand; the other two, set on poles, are waist-high to a mounted man. (Illustration by David Joseph Wright)

– it was the epitome of martial flow. Moreover, the culture of flamboyance and panache that these exercises promoted surely transferred to the battlefield. Bearing witness to such outstanding skills must have been daunting to the average soldier – the horse-archer was a formidable and glamourous foe. When contests exhibiting this level of skill, flourish and excitement were held at the *ok meidan*, they drew large crowds of enthusiastic onlookers. They celebrated the art of the horse-archer and elevated his status in society.

The Manchu track

As late as the 19th century, a Chinese Jesuit priest, Étienne Zie, recorded details of an ongoing tradition of horse-archery trials in Qing Dynasty China. These proceedings were a component of formal military examinations. Eager to perpetuate the proud heritage of nomadic fighting arts, the Manchu emperors had long promoted horse-archer skills in the army. It helped to forge a distinct Manchurian identity and to rally the fighting spirit of the horse-archer class with a sense of exceptionalism.

Zie recounts that the elementary-level examination for the military required the candidate to ride a course, which commenced with a curving section into the straight, and to shoot at three targets. The archer started out with both a bow and a single arrow in his left hand, and carried a further two arrows stowed in his belt. In these respects the exercise resembles the present-day Korean three-shot course, as contested in International competition.

It differed greatly, however, with regard to the distance between the targets and the necessity for rapid shooting. The modern track is 90 yards, with just 30 yards between targets. The best archers on the fastest horses do this, and hit all three marks, in around 7 seconds; others take as long as 9 seconds. By *furūsiyya* standards – shooting at ten targets placed a mere 7 yards apart, on horses of equivalent speed – the modern track would appear leisurely. However, the Manchu elementary track was an even less hurried excursion. It extended a massive 335 yards, with targets placed almost 100 yards apart. The most common form of target was the 'heaven-man-and-earth target', which consisted of a rolled rattan mat, standing

8 feet high, wrapped in white paper and marked with three circles. Two small pennants fluttered on top to indicate wind direction, though this was of negligible significance given that the targets were placed just 6 feet from the outer edge of the low, earth embankment that flanked the track (Selby 2000: 355).

It would seem that there was a different emphasis for the novice Qing horse-archer than for the elite *fāris* at the height of his skills. Being able to shoot successive arrows quickly was not a requirement; neither was being able to shoot a great distance. This really was beginner's stuff, although the targets were probably fairly narrow columns (their diameter is not recorded) and so flashing by on a quick horse required careful timing to land the shot. Amusingly, Zie adds that 'the local hotheads always try to grab the arrows in full flight, resulting in varying degrees of injury' (Selby 2000: 351). We might deduce that, for this to be even remotely possible, the cadets were using lightweight bows, as recommended in the early stages of training by all archery cultures.

Manchus who were born into banner households (hereditary military families) were trained in archery and horsemanship from an early age; few bannermen were required to take these entry-level tests. The elementary military examinations were primarily a route for other Chinese, of a non-military background, to enter or to advance in the Qing army. Since these candidates were not destined to be high-calibre troops, lightweight bows were appropriate for their expected abilities. Commanders frequently complained about the poor quality of troops enlisted via this system. Elite Manchu horse-archers were more likely to display their proficiency in the hunting field and to shoot powerful bows.

Mogu

In Korea, horse-archers trained not only by shooting at targets along a track but also by taking part in an exciting hunt-related contest called *mogu*. The *mogu* was a large wickerwork ball, about 3 feet in diameter, covered in canvas. It was towed by means of a rope behind a galloping lead horse. Horse-archers rode after it in competing pairs. Their blunt arrows, having been dipped in some form of dye, registered hits with splotches of their respective colour. Though appearing more like a rehearsal for hunting, pursuit games like this were of equal value to the military archer.

Exhibition shots

In *Arab Archery* a variety of challenging shots are listed, from shooting out the flames of candles to a boomerang shot, which involved shooting an arrow, nocked and fletched at each end with four feathers and having a lead weight inserted at one end only. Perhaps the most ambitious was to be performed from the back of a galloping horse. For this shot, the archer took a blunt wooden arrow, flared at the end but with no head, and shot it at a sword planted in the ground. The objective was to split the arrow (Faris & Elmer 1945: 134–38).

Ambidextrous archers

There is a passage in the Bible, referring to a cadre of elite warriors in the service of King David (r. 1010–970 BC), which states that they could 'shoot arrows with the left hand or the right' (I Chronicles 12: 1–7). Both the account of the entertainment witnessed by William Harborne in Constantinople and the exercise from the *Kitab-i Makbûl der-Hâl-i Huyûl* required shots to both the left and the right. Both sources are specific in reporting that the archers switched their bows from hand to hand accordingly.

It is quite awkward for a right-handed archer to shoot on the right-hand side of the horse. It can be done – indeed it was done – but there is just one fairly narrow forward angle that anatomy will allow in this attitude. The ability to switch the bow to the opposite hand makes it possible to shoot at all angles, which clearly has a military advantage.

Chinese archery literature contains a number of references to the desirability for horse-archers to be able to shoot with both left and right hands. In *The Archery Manual of Li Chengfen* the old master declares, 'If you want to learn horseback archery you have to learn to shoot with either hand, you have to shoot ambidextrously before you can achieve anything' (quoted in Selby 2000: 305–06). He goes on to say that you're in trouble if the enemy comes at you from the wrong side.

Several portraits of warrior nobles from Mughal India depict them with an archer's ring on each thumb (Koppedrayer 2002: 32), suggesting that they were proficient at shooting a bow with either hand. It is an idea supported in a Sanskrit treatise on Dhanurveda (the art and science of archery) written by Vasistha in the 17th century, but drawing from much earlier teachings, which also advocated the necessity of being able to shoot with either hand (Ray 2014: 28).

I have recently been teaching myself to shoot left-handed. Although awkward at first, it is becoming easier and I have similar accuracy (and inaccuracy) to my right-handed shooting. Although I cannot yet pull an equally heavy bow left-handed, there is no reason why that wouldn't be attainable with training.

THE HORSE-ARCHER: ANGLES OF SHOT

The most convenient and usual shots for the right-handed horse-archer were either to shoot forwards to the left of the horse's neck or directly to the left-hand side. These provided good attack opportunities for either approaching or moving along an enemy line. Ambidextrous ability allowed for these positions to be reversed when countering mounted assailants engaging from the opposite side. This still left a number of angles unexploited, however, and two specialized shots bridged the gap.

The Parthian shot

This iconic shooting stance of the horse-archer, in which he turns in the saddle to shoot over his shoulder, has been traditionally ascribed to Parthian origins. The identical shot is evident in art from all cultures, however, including those that pre-date the Parthians; it is seen on Assyrian wall-reliefs, for instance. The Parthian shot is universal to all horse-archer traditions and is as old as horse-archery itself.

An extreme version of the Parthian shot is described in *Arab Archery*, where the archer is enjoined to turn in the saddle with sufficient rotation to shoot to the right of his horse's tail and to aim his arrows at the hoof-prints left by his horse in virgin ground. Its author tells us phlegmatically that such a shot is 'useful in the event that you are followed by a lion … which might hang on to your mount. A shot would disentangle the beast' (Faris & Elmer 1945: 136).

The author demonstrating the Parthian shot – a shot that is synonymous with horse-archer tactics. It involves the archer turning in the saddle to shoot behind. Chiefly, it was used in a feigned retreat that had succeeded in drawing pursuit from enemy cavalry. However, it could also be used in a regular assault against blocks of infantry. The archer shot forwards as he galloped towards a formation. If a column of horse-archers approached at a slight diagonal, then all archers would have the ability to shoot successive shots diagonally forwards from their horses, raking along the enemy line. They could then wheel away on the opposite diagonal and continue to shoot 'Parthian shots' for a distance equal to their approach. (KH)

Parthian horse-archers attack a disrupted line of Roman legionaries (overleaf)

Although this image is not intended to represent the battle of Carrhae (53 BC) specifically, it draws on aspects of that notable engagement, which saw horse-archers deployed to very great effect. Shortly before the moment depicted, the Romans have formed a *testudo* (tortoise) formation as a defence against continuous assaults from horse-archers. In response, the Parthians have sent in their heavy armoured cavalry – the *cataphracts*. Some of these crack-troops and their horses have been struck and skewered by *pila* (javelins) as they drew near. Their corpses litter the Roman front line. A majority of *cataphracts* have managed to crash through, however, disrupting the Roman formation and creating chaos. As they smashed into the shields with their well-armoured horses, they thrust to left and right with their thick spears, using powerful two-handed stabs. They rode through, on and away.

Reeling from the shock of this steel-clad juggernaut, the Romans – mangled, bloody and broken – have attempted to pick themselves up and to reform. At that moment, however, the instant of this image, a tornado of Parthian horse-archers bursts through the thick clouds of dust generated by thousands of clattering hooves on the desert rock. Staying out of reach of the Roman *pila*, which were short-range weapons, the Parthian horse-archers launch wheeling attacks to exploit the Romans' disarray. Injured, scrambling, jostling and without clear commands, the Romans are unable to order their shields quickly enough. This leaves them exposed to arrows more than usual. Aimed shafts find their mark in necks, faces, arms and legs.

Like the Parthian horse-archer portrayed on a stone relief now in the Museum of Islamic Art, Berlin (see page 56), these horse-archers carry spare arrows in their bow-hands. This enables them to shoot extremely rapidly, delivering a burst of arrows as they gallop in and away from their unfortunate quarry. The Parthian shot was as effective in a frontal assault on a line like this, as it was when turning to shoot pursuers in a feinted retreat. It allowed the archer to keep shooting for every second that he was in bowshot of the enemy.

The author demonstrating the *jarmaki*. In his treatise on archery, written in the 14th century, Taybughā described an unusual shooting position, which he called the *jarmaki*. It required the archer to 'bring his right hand up and over his head, tuck his head beneath his right wrist so that his hand rests in the nape of his neck' (quoted in Latham & Paterson 1970: 82). What initially sounds like a challenging contortion becomes reasonably easy to accomplish if, at approximately half-draw, one rotates the bow-arm to be palm uppermost and simultaneously swings the draw-hand behind the neck. Completion of the draw is executed by pushing down with the bow, rather than pulling back with the string. (KH)

Jarmaki

The *jarmaki* required the archer to shoot with his draw-hand behind the head. It enabled a very tight, downwards shot, adjacent to the horse, allowing the archer to shoot at targets that were otherwise unreachable. On the battlefield it may have been used to dispatch fallen foes as the archer rode by during the rout. In the hunt it had the potential to shoot an animal that had been overtaken in pursuit or an animal, such as a lion, that was itself about to pounce at the hindquarters of the horse.

Taybughā also commended the *jarmaki* shot for the infantry archer shooting down from fortifications; it facilitated a shot angle to the base of the wall while minimizing the archer's need to lean over and expose himself to danger. He further proposed the technique for shooting at an enemy hiding in a well (Latham & Paterson 1970: 137).

Speed-shooting

William of Tyre observed in his chronicles of the Crusades that 'The Saracen cavalry … began to shoot thicker and faster than one could believe possible' (quoted in Smail 1995: 76). Being able to shoot successive arrows in rapid bursts was fundamental to the tactics of many horse-archers, who could be in contact with their target for only a few seconds at a time.

There were two main challenges to being able to shoot quickly; the first was the ability to come to full-draw. Qi Jiguang (17th century) advised, 'When you teach mounted archery tell them: "You should ride like the wind … reach full draw and release quickly"' (quoted in Tian &

Ma 2015: 123). Gao Ying agreed with him, noting that failing to reach full draw was a common fault (Tian & Ma 2015:123). With a powerful bow it takes time to draw the string to the ear; it requires every muscle in the body, and such effort is usually engaged gradually. However, on a quick horse there is no time and the draw cannot be compromised or the archer will miss his mark. The real power requirement for a horse-archer is not just that of being able to draw a heavy bow, but in being able to draw it fully in an instant, without tearing or straining muscles.

The second skill to be mastered was the ability to place an arrow on the string in the blink of an eye. Impressively rapid nocking – taking shafts directly from the quiver – was possible, but it did not match the speed of holding a second or third arrow in the hand. *Arab Archery* relates four methods for in-hand shooting (Faris & Elmer 1945: 151–53).

The first was to hold several arrows by the nocks with the three outer fingers of the string-hand folded into the palm – the thumb and index finger were used both to locate the arrow on the string and also to draw and shoot. It seems a precarious grasp, possibly not suitable for the battlefield, but many modern horse-archers achieve remarkable speeds using this method.

An alternative, according to our authority, was to hold the nocks of the arrows between each divide of two fingers, with the arrows extending from the back of the hand. For nine arrows, three arrows in each divide were suggested. Apart from the fact that it is not explained how one then locks the thumb with the index finger for the draw, there is the issue of arrows wagging furiously, and dislodging, when the archer is in motion.

A carving of a Parthian horseman. Note that he carries several arrows in his bow-hand. It is also notable that, despite the fact he rides without stirrups, he is nevertheless angling his torso forward and assuming a posture very similar to that of heavy bow shooters and of horse-archers who use their stirrups to take this position. (© bpk/Museum für Islamische Kunst, SMB /Georg Niedermeiser)

Thirdly, another draw-hand technique, is a method whereby the archer holds the arrows midway on the shaft, with the nocks towards the elbow. I have used this system both from chariots and horseback and, with reed-slim shafts, feel comfortable holding several in the hand securely. It is quite an easy method to master.

Finally, *Arab Archery* refers to the technique of holding arrows in the bow-hand and instantly dismisses it because 'it renders the grip weak' (quoted in Faris & Elmer 1945: 153). This system was also described by Qi Jiguang: 'When you are on horseback, you should hold three arrows. You should hold two of them together with the handle and have one arrow already nocked …' (quoted in Tian & Ma 2015: 122). Gao Ying disagreed with his teaching. He too maintained that holding arrows in the bow-hand rendered the grip unsteady.

This was not a view shared by everyone. An overwhelming majority of images in art that depict in-hand arrows show them in the bow-hand, not the string-hand. An Assyrian wall-relief from Nimrud (c.865 BC) and now in the British Museum depicts an archer on the battlements holding a pair of arrows in his bow-hand and, as already noted, there is an account of the Pharaoh Amenhotep II holding four arrows in this manner.

In the 12th century, Mardi ibn Ali al-Tarsusi, who wrote an important military manual for Saladin, advised: 'If you wish to shoot and have a sword, drop the sword from your right hand, seize the wrist loop and slide it up the forearm. Hold the bow and three arrows in your left hand' (quoted in Nicolle 1994: 52). Clearly, it is easier to manage a sword hanging from your right arm while shooting, if the action of taking the next arrow involves no more than a relatively horizontal back-and-forth movement of the string-hand to reach for arrows from the bow-hand, rather than dropping it vertically behind to take arrows from the quiver.

Moreover, we have the testimony of the *Münyetü'l-Ġuzāt*, which is clear that the archer can shoot with five arrows in his bow-hand as well as his string-hand. Bow-hand carriage is a system favoured by many horse-archers today, including myself. It is fast and it is secure; ideal for competitive and display shooting with relatively lightweight bows. Even so, both the author of *Arab Archery* and Gao Ying had a point – carrying arrows in the bow-hand was a system that had the potential to weaken the grip.

Arab Archery refers to Al-Tabari achieving a burst of 15 successive arrows. Even with the shafts distributed between both hands, this would be too many for a strong bow. Such cumbersome numbers would undoubtedly unsteady the grip. Three in the bow-hand is the maximum for me with lightweight bows (under 60lb) but if a heavier bow were to be used, there would need to be fewer in-hand arrows. With the notable exception of the archer in the Bayeux Tapestry who is carrying four arrows in his bow-hand, the evidence of art is that two or three arrows were the most ever carried in this fashion into combat. It is a number that can be accommodated without compromising the ability for a correct grip. Larger numbers of arrows were carried in-hand on occasion, such as for exhibition shooting, when a lighter draw-weight bow could be used but, for the battlefield, two or three sufficed.

Apart from considerations of grip, there was no necessity for more. A fast-galloping horse covers a considerable distance in a few seconds, and two or three arrows in a sequence of burst-shooting at a particular target before passing it would have been optimal. A further small cluster of arrows could then be drawn swiftly from the quiver.

It is technically possible to hold very large numbers of arrows in the bow-hand, as is the practice among some modern horse-archery enthusiasts, who can manage as many as twelve shafts threaded between their fingers. It is clever and impressive stuff, useful for multiple shots from a slow horse in a competition or for an entertainment display, but of limited military application. Setting up with anything other than a simple clutch of three requires time-consuming and careful digital arrangement that is not compatible with battlefield urgency.

Furthermore, horse-archers were versatile troops, equally adept with sword and mace. The demands of the battlefield might change in an instant and they needed to be able to switch from bow to sidearm in a breath; to be able to take up the reins and draw a sword without the fuss of dropping an excess of valuable ammunition. Retrieving the reins remains possible with only one or two arrows in the bow-hand (which is also the rein hand) but not with a bouquet of shafts. With regard to the string-hand (which is also the sword hand), it was more prudent, on the battlefield, to leave that unencumbered.

Details of a wall-relief depicting the Assyrian King Ashurbanipal hunting. Note the ring on the thumb of the bow-hand, serving as an arrow-shelf. Ashurbanipal rides bareback, save for a textured saddle-cloth. He does not rise to shoot. He is taking a difficult shot on the off-side of the horse. Both he and his attendant are wearing shoulder-quivers and the attendant has a pair of arrows at the ready to pass to his master, indicative that the archer might hold an additional arrow in-hand in order to be able to make a rapid second shot at his prey. Similar images showing him hunting on foot also include an attendant passing him a pair of arrows. (Werner Forman)

INFANTRY ARCHERS: TRAINING AND PRACTICE

Even for the infantry archer, shooting the composite bow required a range of shooting techniques and modes. Vasistha, in his *Dhanurveda Samhita*, offers high praise to the archer who can pierce two wooden balls thrown into the air at the same time. He generously gave the option for the archer either to pierce both with one shot, or to be fast enough to get a single shot off at each (Ray 2014: 41). Although this may seem an improbable feat for the average archer, it highlighted the importance of training to be able to hit moving targets. Vasistha went on to decree that archery on foot should also be practised while running; this underlined the fact that, during combat, the archer himself may be on the move.

For the Qing military examinations candidates were required to shoot at six roughly man-size targets. Originally these targets were placed at 135 yards – quite a distance for a heavy Manchu arrow. After 1693 the distance was reduced to 84 yards and eventually, after 1760, to 50 yards.

There was also a seventh target – a leather ball, lacquered bright red. This was set in a mound of earth. In his eyewitness account Étienne Zie compares it to a pumpkin standing around 2 feet tall and about 1 foot in diameter. He doesn't say, but I would guess that it was filled with seeds or grains to give it some weight. This was an exercise in delivering 'thump'. Zie notes that 'the candidate not only has to touch the ball; he must knock it out of the supporting hummock' (Selby 2000: 353).

We are not told the distance for the ball shot, but Zie does mention that to accomplish this feat, the archer used a hefty arrow armed with a leather blunt some 2½ inches in diameter. That is a heavy missile that could only have been delivered with the requisite force from a reasonably heavy bow. Qualification depended on only three of the seven targets being hit.

A Safavid Persian treatise, *Jāme al-Hadāyat fi Elm al-Romāyat* (*The Complete Guide Concerning the Science of Archery*), written around 1575, advocated being able to shoot both standing and sitting (kneeling): 'When sitting, one keeps the sole of the right foot flat on the ground as is natural and keeps the right knee erect. He kneels on the left knee and sits on the heel of the left foot' (Khorasani 2013: 79). Such practices were useful for the front rank of an in-depth formation of archers, or in topography where it benefited the archer to stay low to the ground or remain concealed behind a natural feature.

Justin Ma (co-author of *The Way of Archery*) demonstrating the immaculate and elegant form of Gao Ying's teachings, aligning the skeleton in the optimal manner for mechanical efficiency, and thus reducing the stresses on muscle and tendon. Ancient teachings in all archery cultures placed emphasis on perfecting form before either increasing the draw-weight of the bow or shooting at faraway targets. (ML)

Arab Archery describes the practice of shooting blindfolded in the direction of a sound (Faris & Elmer 1945: 134), a technique also recommended by Vasistha, who explained that an assistant throws stones at a bronze vessel to create the target acoustic (Ray 2014: 43). Such ability obviously had its advantages in the event of a night raid, though it was perhaps of equal risk to friend and foe.

More prosaically, archery training began with a close-range target, a lightweight bow and the perfection of form. Close-range targets in all cultures were similar – from the Turkish *torba* to the Chinese *gaozhen*. Consisting of either densely packed wood-shavings in a sack or tightly bundled straw, they were barrel-shaped and shot end-on, receiving arrows shot from only a few feet away. The angle that an arrow struck the target revealed faults in the form of the release – a clean loose would result in the arrow sticking in perpendicular to the target. Technique had to be

Ice-skating Manchu archers are depicted during a performance for the Qianlong Emperor (r. 1735–96) during Chinese New Year on Houhai Lake in Beijing. Ice-skating divisions of archers were deployed in northern campaigns because they could move swiftly over frozen rivers. The figure under the arch is shooting up at the target suspended from the arch with a shot that combines elements of the *qabac* with the Parthian shot. (Image courtesy of The Palace Museum, Beijing)

59

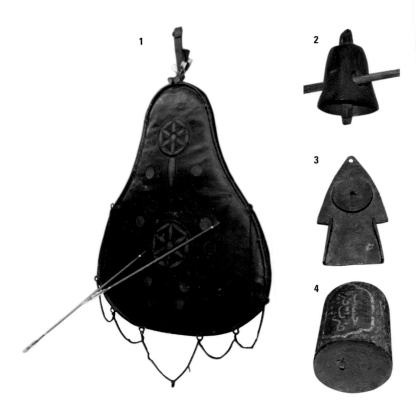

Turkish targets. The puta (**1**) is made from leather and stuffed with cottonseeds. The curious pear shape probably represented the face-on profile of a man on a horse, with the swell of the lower half suggesting the form of a man's legs astride the animal. These targets manifested in several sizes, but the largest approximated to the size of a man. When suspended from a wooden frame, with the top of the target above the ground to the height of a mounted man, it offered target practice at approaching cavalry. Intended to be shot at long range, this example has bells affixed to it to let a distant shooter know that he had struck. The precise scoring system is not known, but clearly there were zones for both man and horse, which may have scored differently. Darb targets served to demonstrate the penetrating power of the bow. These ranged from polished metal plates in frames (like mirrors) that were held up by nervous servants, to ploughshares, bells and blocks of wood. These examples in Istanbul's Military Museum show a pierced bell (**2**); a ploughshare that has been penetrated (**3**) and a very dense log of wood that was shot by Hasib Ziya in 1719 (**4**). (Image courtesy of the Military Museum, Harbiye-Istanbul)

perfected before stepping outside to aim at more distant targets.

Targets were even more varied than the types of composite bow that existed. In many instances the target was no more than a mound of earth or a block of clay, softened with water prior to shooting. These wet-clay targets could be shot with either sharps or blunts. More elaborate were panniers of sand or coils of straw, covered with a painted canvas. A particularly distinctive type of Ottoman target was a stuffed leather bag called a *puta*. All these butts were devised to permit the practice of accurate shooting. Another type of target, known as a *darb*, was used to test penetration.

Different cultures placed varying emphasis on the size and the penetrability of targets. In Turkey and in Persia, chief among the archery arts was the quest to shoot for the longest-possible range. An ultimate demonstration of the power of the composite bow, this exercise was known as flight-shooting.

FLIGHT-SHOOTING

On 9 July 1794 the Secretary to the Turkish Ambassador to London, Mahmud Effendi, impressed onlookers gathered in a field behind Bedford Square by shooting an arrow a distance of 482 yards (Heath 1971: 79). We are not told in which direction the shot was made, but it is tempting to think that the arrow may have landed within the footprint of what is

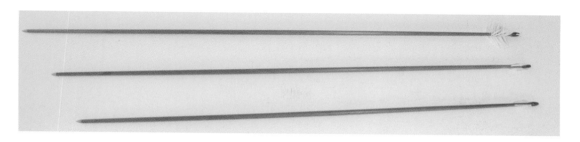

now the British Museum, which lies adjacent. The spectators included members of the Royal Toxophilite Society, and Effendi – who had been made an honorary member of the society in 1794 – complained to them that the grounds were too restricted for what he would consider a long shot. The area had a number of established buildings and was not entirely open space. Effendi was merely demonstrating the techniques of the flight-shooter, not claiming his shot to be any great distance by Turkish standards. The bow and arrow used on the occasion are preserved in the society's collection at Archer's Hall in Buckinghamshire.

Just a few years later, in 1798, the Sultan Selim III drove an arrow into the ground at a distance of 972 yards (Heath 1971: 79). That was more like it. By the 18th century, flight-shooting had become a Turkish passion – some would say obsession. In order to achieve these impressive distances, special equipment was used. First the bows were of tremendous power, but more significantly, special arrows and techniques were employed.

Arrows needed to be as light and aerodynamic as possible. Flight arrows were much shorter than regular arrows. This reduced their overall mass, meaning they required less energy to propel them, and also minimized the amount of air resistance that they encountered. These diminutive, needle-like shafts required a special piece of equipment in order to shoot them – a *sipur*. Such tiny projectiles, fitted with minimal fletching, were capable of being shot over a vast distance and obviously required a clear landscape in order to be able to find them. Today, the world flight-shooting championships are held on the salt flats of Utah, for obvious reasons.

Following the Turkish conquest of Constantinople in 1453, an archer's guild was formed in the city. It established a famous shooting ground called the *ok meidan*. Kani mentions numerous other cities throughout the Islamic world where similar shooting grounds existed. These included Mecca, Alexandria, Damascus, Gallipoli, Belgrade, Baghdad and Cairo (Klopsteg 1987: 107). At the *ok meidan*, spectators would enjoy all manner of archery events, shaded in luxurious tents and lounging on sumptuous cushions. The chief attraction, however, was always flight-

Replica flight arrows in the author's collection. Flight arrows were constructed to be as light and slender as possible in order to minimize the slowing effects of friction and drag. The thinner you make an arrow, however, the more you reduce its 'spine' – its stiffness. An arrow of insufficient spine will not stand in a heavy bow; it will break. In order to counteract this, flight arrows were barrelled – made thicker in the centre and tapered towards the ends. This profile increased the stiffness of the shaft, while making it as light as possible. The middle arrow is feather-fletched and the bottom arrow, parchment-fletched. These tiny vanes provide the necessary stability at the cost of minimal drag. The top arrow is an *abrish*, used in practice. (Today, an arrow with this arrangement is called a 'flu-flu', after the onomatopoeic 'floo-hoo', a word employed by the Seminole Indians to describe a very broad-fletched arrow used for hunting small game at close quarters; Maurice Thompson recorded its use (Thompson 1878: 202).) The spiral fletching of the *abrish* created drag, causing it to fly slower and for less distance. This not only made it easier to recover but, most importantly, observers were able to track its flight pattern and advise the archer of any refinements he should make to his technique. (KH)

A *sipur*. This device, strapped to the wrist of the bow-hand and separate from the bow, acts as an arrow-shelf. It extends to within the bow and allows an 'overdraw' – that is to say, a short arrow may be taken to full draw by allowing it to be pulled back to within the radius of the bow's arc. It is used in flight-shooting. The *Münyetü' l-Ġuzāt* extols the virtues of shooting with such a device: 'This is a good skill to shoot at the people in high fortresses and the people who are far away and for many other things. Because an arrow like this travels a long distance; it travels about one thousand arshins [roughly 775 yards] and even more, they say' (Öztopçu 1986: 198). Vasistha commented that arrows shot with the *nalika* (a similar device used in India) 'can be shot a great distance from a high place and are especially useful in siege craft' (Ray 2014: 21). (Image courtesy of the Military Museum, Harbiye-Istanbul)

shooting. In parts of Turkey, particularly Istanbul, exquisitely carved stone pillars that were erected to mark shots of significant distance may still be seen today.

There were four classes of members in the Constantinople Guild: 'the Seniors', 'the 900s', 'the 1000s', and 'the 1100s'. These numbers represented the distance, measured in *gez* (100 gez = 68 yards), that had been attained by a particular class of archer (Klopsteg 1987: 107). In yards we might call them the 610-yard men, the 680-yard men and the 750-yard men. There were also 820-yard men ('the 1200s'), but they were of such exceptional ability that they apparently didn't warrant an officially assigned class of their own. Doubtless such rare beings enjoyed celebrity by dint of their individual name rather than by mere guild qualification. An archer continually had to prove his ability to shoot at a designated distance: failure to do so meant that he was downgraded.

In my book *The Longbow* (Loades 2013 : 33) I posited that a possible reason for Henry VIII's injunctions for archers to be able to shoot a certain distance (280 yards) was not necessarily because great range was required on the battlefield, but because it was a way of measuring an archer's ability to draw a bow of adequate military power. Today we calibrate bows according to draw-weight, but doing so according to their ability to propel an arrow of known weight a certain distance seems an equally good measure. Moreover, it combines this with an indication of the archer's ability to deliver the full power of his bow with good shooting technique.

The composite bow in Western Europe

In a sequence depicting the Norman attack at the battle of Hastings (1066), the Bayeux Tapestry represents a number of infantry archers in Duke William's army using composite bows. A group of four is shown in the main panel in support of charging cavalry and a further 23 appear in the lower border. The bows have been portrayed crudely, but they are short and there is enough suggestion of the signature recurve shape to be confident with this identification. In a separate section, the tapestry illustrates a horse-archer, amid other cavalry, pressing home the rout.

The infantry archers are shown shooting with a chest-draw and, for the most part, doing so while running forwards in the attack. Their recruitment and presence has not been chronicled, but there were strong links between the Norman/Norse world and the Varangians. The Varangians formed an eastern branch of Viking expansion and settlement, centred upon Kiev, where they would have encountered the composite bow. Furthermore, crack Varangian troops served as the bodyguard of the Byzantine Emperor in Constantinople. Harald Hardrada, who invaded the north of

England a few days prior to William's landings in the south, was formerly a commander of the Varangian Guard, and it is possible that he recruited some elite archers from the East to support this adventure. If so, it is not inconceivable that, following his defeat at Stamford Bridge (1066), these soldiers of fortune might have raced south and gained employment with Duke William.

It is equally possible that they were homegrown troops. Carolingian art, from the late 8th century to the end of the 10th century, is plentifully populated with images of archers shooting composite bows. Between the 8th and 10th centuries the Franks, with whom the Normans assimilated, had waged frequent wars on their eastern borders against the Avars and Magyars. These fierce horse-archers introduced them to the composite bow and it appears that, up until the Norman invasion of England, the composite bow was well established and widely used by the warrior class in Western Europe. Archaeologically, the bone laths that buttressed the grip and *siyahs* of Hunnic-type bows have been found extensively throughout Western Europe and Scandinavia.

This detail from the Bayeux Tapestry shows infantry archers using composite bows with a characteristic recurve shape. Note that one of the archers wears a shoulder-quiver, while the others wear belt-quivers. One archer is holding four arrows in his bow-hand. All the archers are shooting while running. (DEA / M. SEEMULLER)

ARROW TYPES

A bewildering array of arrows was shot from the composite bow. They carried many different styles of arrowhead and displayed diverse forms of shaft, nock and fletching. Space does not permit a comprehensive study, but some of the more ingenious and unusual varieties call out to be mentioned.

Rocket arrows pre-date and are distinct from incendiary arrows. Shortly after the invention of gunpowder in the 9th century AD, the Chinese launched firework-like rockets by means of an arrow. The arrow provided the propulsion to direct the missile, with reasonable accuracy, towards a target area. Before the end of its flight the fuse of the rocket ignited and the resulting firecracker dance of flame, smoke and noise caused terrified panic among enemy horses. If it was to ignite in the air, where it created maximum impact and confusion, a rocket arrow had to be shot neither too early, nor too late. I have shot a replica of one of these contraptions and they demand very careful timing!

Incendiary arrows had obvious advantages for naval warfare in an age of wooden ships, and for besiegers wishing to fire a town. Various types existed, ranging from the Korean *hwajeon*, which consisted of rolled linen and paper impregnated with a black-powder compound and coated with resin, to a tar-soaked, straw-and-cotton ball inserted into a fire-basket arrow as advocated by the author of *Arab Archery* (Faris & Elmer 1945: 134) That author also goes on to cite a mixture of otter fat, wax, black sulphur, cherry seeds and a tree resin similar to myrrh that was kneaded together with balsam oil. It received an additive of quicklime. Once dry, the hardened paste was ground into granules. Apparently, this amalgam required no pre-ignition, but burst into flames as it travelled through the air.

Arguably, the most impressive type of incendiary arrow was that described by Taybughā (Latham & Paterson 1970: 140). It involved draining an egg and filling it with naphtha. This – now-flammable – egg was inserted into the wide, open end of a cone mounted at the fore-end of the arrow. Prior to introducing the egg, a red-hot iron pellet was located in the narrow neck of the cone. The angle of the cone was such that the egg could not come into direct contact with the iron pellet in the resting position, provided that the device was held at an upward angle. The arrow, unfletched, was tied to the string by its nock and steadied at the forward end by a loop around the grip of the bow. When shot, the blunt head of the arrow acted as a ram, pushing through the cone, forcing the pellet into the egg and igniting it. At the same

Arrows with whistling heads were a particular feature of Chinese archery. These examples dating to the Han Dynasty are made from iron. Wood, bone and horn were also common materials. Primarily they served to flush game in the hunting field. They were also used for battlefield communication, as signalling arrows. An early written reference occurs in the *Annals of Sima Qian* (*c.*109 BC): 'Miedun then made whistling arrows and drilled his troops in their use' (Liao Wanzhen 1999). In the din of battle shouted commands were often futile, and valuable time could be lost in relaying messages from a commander to individual troop captains. Seizing the optimal moment to strike was equally as important as deciding where to strike. A commander could direct a troop by shooting a whistling arrow at precisely where he wished a strike to land. Its shrill pitch could be distinguished from the roar, stamp and clash of battle. Used in particular with cavalry, a whistle signal produced an instant response at the moment of a commander's decision. An enhancement was to use a whistle and incendiary arrow combination, producing both an audible and a visual signal. (Photograph courtesy of the Dunhuang Museum)

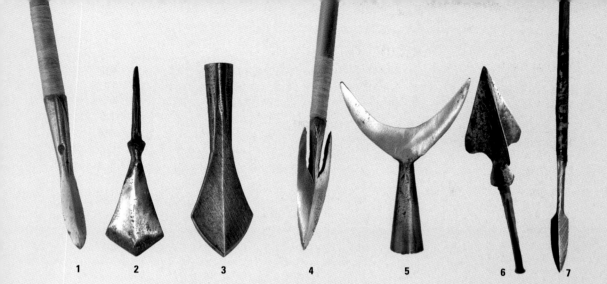

1   2   3   4   5   6   7

Arrowheads

Although there are literally hundreds of different styles of arrowhead used with the composite bow, three are among the most common.

The bodkin-style head (**1**) was intended primarily for attacking metal armour; the four-sided head is slender but, having curved edges, is very tough structurally.

Slight variations on the lozenge-shaped head (**2** and **3**) occurred in all cultures where the composite bow flourished, and it was the most common type used for war, possessing the optimal angles of cutting edge for attacking leather armour. The two examples here also show the two systems for fitting an arrowhead to the shaft. Arrowheads were either fabricated with a tang that inserted into the arrow (**2**), or made with a tapered socket that fitted over the shaft (**3**). Tanged arrowheads were ideal for bamboo arrows, but were also widely used on wooden shafts. Heating the tang until red hot and using it to bore a hole in the shaft created a tight custom fit. The shaft, whether bamboo or wood, was then tightly bound with thread to maintain compression.

The barbed arrowhead (**4**) was especially suitable for attacking unarmoured horses. Penetration would lead to extensive bleeding. The barbs prevented it from being dislodged easily, so that it would wag in the wound and cause havoc-creating pain for the poor animal. Slender barbed arrowheads were also slight enough and sharp enough to have some impact against poor-quality armour at close range.

The crescent-headed arrow (**5**) was common in all cultures and generally considered to be for shooting small game or birds. There is an intriguing passage in Vasistha's *Dhanurveda Samhita*, however, that refers to the 'two bladed arrow with the little curved fist' shooting enemy arrows out of the air, going on to state that 'If the archer cuts off the enemy's arrows with the help of his own arrows, then he will be proclaimed as 'arrow breaker' (Ray 2014: 40). If such a feat were possible, it probably depended upon the archer being stationed a little forward and on the flanks of his own army and shooting across the line.

First appearing during the Bronze Age and common throughout the Classical World, the trilobate arrowhead (**6**) consisted of three blades. Although they offered a greater challenge to manufacture than a normal double-bladed broadhead, these nasty little points were a source of terror on the battlefield. It was especially difficult to staunch the flow of blood from a trilobate arrowhead, because it created what surgeons today refer to as a star wound – it was significantly more difficult to stitch together the resulting multiple flaps of skin.

The Manchu plum-needle arrow (**7**) was the most widely used form of arrowhead for Qing warfare. The sharp cutting edges of the head, made from folded steel, taper into a sturdy shank. This gave both weight and minimal resistance to allow penetration to a fatal depth. Extending from the shank on the example shown here is a tang that embeds into the bamboo shaft, which is bound at this point with a cherry-bark wrap to prevent splitting. (All photos courtesy KH)

Although some short arrows could be shot with a *sipur*, darts (less than half the length of a normal arrow) required a more elaborate apparatus – an arrow-guide, known variously as a *mijrat* or *navek*. Here, Dodo Tanyer demonstrates the use of a replica *navek*. The wooden guide, which has two holes drilled at the nock end, is tied to the string, so that it is retained after the shot. On release, the string moves both arrow and guide forward until the string comes to rest; the arrow then travels along the guide before exiting and continuing its flight. An amount of energy is lost owing to the mass and friction of the guide, though much of this is compensated for because the smaller arrow has less air resistance to overcome. Short arrows were commonly used during sieges to avoid supplying the enemy with regular ammunition. (Photograph courtesy of Cemal Hünal)

time it launched the egg as a ball of fire. Taybughā alludes to it being used at the siege of Acre – probably the second siege in 1291, in which Baybars al-Bunduqdari fielded multiple batteries of trebuchets (Latham & Paterson 1970: 143). A common defence against trebuchet barrage was to suspend thick bales of cotton over targeted areas to buffer the shock; incendiary arrows were an ideal means of countering these great cushions.

Seeking ways to render shot arrows unusable to the enemy was a common challenge. In his account of the siege of Adrianople (AD 378), Ammianus Marcellinius describes a simple measure – **severed binding**. This allowed regular arrows to be doctored in such a way as to render them useless to an enemy: 'So an order was given that the thongs binding the arrowheads to the shafts should be partially cut through before shooting. This did not affect them in flight, and if they found their mark they were as effective as ever but if they missed they at once fell to pieces' (Marcellinius 1986: 441). The type of arrowheads being used here were fitted into the shaft by means of a tang. In order to keep a tanged arrow securely in place, the end of the shaft was bound tightly with thread.

The use of **poison arrows** seems to be universal to all composite-bow cultures. Each had their own recipes, usually a cocktail of various plants, but one example from Persia involved the bones of a dead cow, buffalo or jackass. These were steeped in a porridge of jackass urine and dung for a period of time, until the bones 'became fat and poisonous' (Khorasani 2013: 59). These toxic bones were then carved into arrowheads. A sliver of bone was likely to remain in the body, even if the victim was able to remove the arrow.

Unique to the use of the composite bow in India was an iron arrow, called the *naraca*; this antique example is in the author's collection. The skill in its manufacture is extraordinary. There is no perceivable join and yet the shaft swells towards the nock, which has been made to resemble a bulbous nock. Only the arrowhead, with razor-sharp edges, has been forge-welded in place. Once it had cut through, there would be almost no friction generating resistance to the heavy but fine, bodkin-like shaft. An iron arrow was heavier than a wooden arrow and so also delivered considerable kinetic energy. Moreover, its slender shaft could stitch through a body as effortlessly as a needle. Vasistha advises that the *naraca* requires five feathers to stabilize it, and also notes that only strong and skilled archers could use it (Ray 2014: 21). Clearly, the *naraca* necessitated a bow with a heavy draw-weight to launch it. (KH)

Shafts, nocks and fletchings

Arrowshafts were either of wood – birch was the most common choice – bamboo or river cane. Lightweight bamboo or cane shafts could be given more weight, and thus deliver more wallop, by being fitted with a wooden foreshaft (**1**); the examples shown here are replica Egyptian arrows made by Edward McEwen. Note the different types of bronze arrowhead, which have been mounted on the acacia-wood foreshafts. These foreshafts also provided a strong union at the junction with the arrowhead. If the arrow snapped here on impact, which arrows were prone to do on very light shafts, it reduced the energy delivered to the target. Maintaining the weight and directional force of the arrowshaft behind the head enhanced the power of the punch. The bottom arrow of the four is fitted only with a foreshaft of sharpened ebony; against unarmoured opponents or for hunting small game, such arrows were equally effective as those with a metal head.

Nocks were very often bulbous. This not only made them strong but also exaggerated the feel of the nock in the fingers, and that was an advantage when orienting the notch to the string with blind-nocking techniques – essential for speed-shooting. On wooden arrows a bulbous nock was usually made by laminating shaped slivers of either hardwood or horn to the sides of the shaft at the nock (**2**). The whole was then bound with sinew or other strong thread and glued. When dry, the notch of the nock was cut to bisect both the wood and the binding. Bulbous nocks could also be produced by taking a larger shaft and carving them before reducing the main length of the arrow to the required diameter. This was a highly skilled process that might also involve shaping the shaft to be either bob-tailed or barrelled. For bamboo or cane shafts, bulbous nocks were carved as separate pieces from a different material such as wood, horn, ivory or bone.

A particular problem in siege warfare was that when shooting into fortifications, the attacking force inadvertently replenished a supply of ammunition that the defenders might otherwise exhaust. The opposite case was equally true. One solution was the use of the nockless arrow, requiring a specific device fitted to the string to enable them to be shot (**3**). Taybughā recommended the *julbah*, a tubular contrivance into which the coned end of the arrow inserted (Latham & Paterson 1970: 139); the arrow could not be shot back without the enemy possessing a similar device. The author of *Arab Archery* suggested a *birun* – a ring fitted with a spike – that was also attached to the string. A hole was bored in the end of the arrow and this located onto the spike (Faris & Elmer 1945: 133).

Another type shot using a *julbah* was the razor-nock arrow (**4**). In the frenzy of battle an enemy might retrieve such an arrow and attempt to shoot it back. If he did not notice the concealed blade (polished here to highlight it for photography) it had the capacity to cut the bowstring, with the consequent potential to destroy the bow. I have also shot this type of arrow successfully, protecting the string with a piece of stout quill. A quill is an item that an archer might have about his person, and is therefore an expedient measure if the hidden blade has been detected.

A chief function of Manchu archery was to deliver a massive whack of kinetic energy at short range; shown here (**5**) is the ray-skin-covered nock of a high-status Manchu arrow built by Jaap Koppedrayer. Larger, longer fletchings helped to stabilize the heavy arrow quickly after leaving the bow, so that it could be accurate at closer distances. However, because these fletchings were longer than the brace-height of a bow, there was a risk of the feathers becoming dishevelled during the drawing process. Consequently, an archer needed to hold the arrow on the string by the nock alone, for a moment of pre-draw to clear the feathers beyond the bow limbs, before he could settle the shaft against the side of the bow. The rough surface provided by the ray-skin assisted in the secure handling of these heavy arrows during this process, especially when in motion on horseback. It also served to reinforce the nock, which was done by other bindings when ray-skin was not available. (All photos courtesy KH)

ARROW CARRIAGE

After detailing the Scythian method for scalping and tanning the scalp skin – these macabre trophies were hung as a 'hand-towels' from the horse harness – Herodotus (5th century BC) reported that 'Many too take off the skin, nails and all, from their dead enemies' right hands and make coverings for their quivers' (Herodotus 2013: 618). Styles of quiver were as wide-ranging as types of bow. Images in art of Achaemenid Persians depict outsize shoulder-quivers, capped with a lid and capable of carrying more than a couple of dozen arrows. The author of *Arab Archery* also describes a type of shoulder-quiver, stating that it should hold between 25 and 30 arrows, although he adds that 'One should not, however, limit himself to that number in battle, but should carry others stuck in his boots up to the feathers and others stuck in his belt' (Faris & Elmer 1945: 155).

In the Bayeux Tapestry one of the composite-bow infantry archers in Duke William's invasion force is shown wearing a shoulder-quiver, although the other 26 wear quivers slung from the waist-belt (see page 63). Nevertheless, a majority of quivers used with the composite bow were worn on the hip. Some quivers were deep, reaching up to the feathers, to prevent arrows falling out during vigorous movement. Others were extremely short, enclosing no more than the lower third of an arrow. Folds of felt lining these quivers enabled the arrows to be held securely. Shorter quivers were favoured by horse-archers in particular because they enabled arrows to be withdrawn much more quickly and ergonomically than from a deeper quiver.

Many composite-bow cultures employed closed quivers, which were usually augmented with a leather flap or cover at the opening. The principal advantage of these closed quivers was to protect the arrows from the elements when on campaign. In use they also offered the opportunity for an archer to select a particular type of arrowhead by feel. The design is such that it is easy to feel the heads and withdraw them without any risk of the hand being pricked by the top of the arrow – even at the flat-out gallop. Any unwelcome rattle from carrying arrows in so solid a receptacle can easily be overcome by inserting a sheepskin plug at the mouth – I have tried such a device and it is no hindrance to drawing shafts swiftly and smoothly.

The 14th-century Mamluk training manual *Nihāyat al-su'l wa l-umniyya fi ta'līm a'mal al-furūsiyya* suggested an additional use for these drum-taut containers. It advised that

19th-century Manchu quiver in a private collection. Although the cross-straps at the front are a later Mongolian/Tibetan influence, the proportions and organization of this quiver are otherwise reminiscent of a Manchu type. The large bows of the Manchu required correspondingly large arrows, and these needed to be stabilized by large fletchings. Manchu quivers allowed the shafts to be fanned, keeping individual arrows spaced to prevent crushing. A sheet of felt was folded into several tight layers and arrows were wedged securely between the folds. The felt held the arrows sufficiently tightly, even for a galloping horseman, to allow for the quiver to be very short. A short quiver enabled a very fast draw. Additionally, Manchu quivers were fitted with pockets that hinged to the rear and slits that created compartments at the front (here substituted by the cross-straps). Both the rear pockets and the front compartments accommodated arrows with a different head to those in the main partition. These may be any number of specialty arrowheads either for hunting or for war. It was an ingenious system. Similar types were common in Mongolia, Tibet and Korea. (Photograph courtesy of Peter Dekker)

anyone wishing to ascertain the proximity of an enemy should 'place it on the ground and lay your head against it, and thus you can hear the sound of hooves or of feet' (quoted in Nicolle 2001: 47).

Loading a closed quiver had its challenges, if the feathers were not to be ruffled. The solution, as seen in art, was to encase the fletched ends of a cluster of arrows in a silk bag. This enabled the entire sheaf to be inserted without damage. Individual arrows drew from this silk wrap without resistance or damage. We may imagine that resupply sheaves of arrows, carried by pack animals, were already parcelled in these linings, and that they could be put in place as quickly as a magazine of rifle cartridges.

A Turkish bow from the 16th or 17th century with its bow-case, known as a *gorytos*, and matching quiver. Both the bow-case and quiver have been fabricated in leather and covered with red velvet featuring silver relief embroidery and with silver sequins. Both were suspended from a belt at the archer's waist, of equal use to the infantry and to the horse-archer. For a right-handed archer the *gorytos* was worn on the left hip and the quiver sat on the right hip. The *gorytos* might carry some additional arrows. Bow-cases and quivers were frequently made en suite and with showy materials – exotic animal skins; fine velvets; damask silks encrusted with rich embroidery or richly tooled fine leathers. In Arabia, Turkey and Persia were to be found quivers of brightly coloured leather, faced entirely with an intricate tracery of metal – usually silver – fretwork. Even on relatively everyday campaign quivers, it was usual, in most cultures, to adorn them with a liberal scattering of metal furnishings cast in gold, silver or bronze. These resplendent and gorgeous accoutrements, 'military bling', indicted both the status and swagger of the wearer and the great value he placed on archery. (© Staatliche Kunstsammlungen, Dresden, Jürgen Karpinski)

IMPACT
Different bows for different blows

Recalling his experiences at the battle of Arsuf (1189), Saladin's biographer, Ibn Shaddād, wrote: 'I saw foot soldiers with as many as ten arrows in their backs, who marched on just as usual without breaking rank' (quoted in Verbruggen 1997: 235). The Byzantine princess Anna Komnene, writing half a century earlier, reported an incident in which 'the arrow did not fly in vain from his hand, but pierced through the long shield and cleft its way through the corselet of mail so that arm and side were pinned together' (Komnene 2009: 288). These testimonies – one hailing the effectiveness of armour; the other a salute to the potency of the bow – are apt to leave us confused. There are many other instances of conflicting accounts. Advocates for the superiority of the one over the other can select texts at will to advance whatever argument they are predisposed to favour.

The composite bow was not a universally standard weapon, however. There was an enormous disparity in draw-weights, in arrow types, in armour styles and in tactical applications. Variations in any one of these elements could affect the outcome and thus evidence, which at first seems contradictory, can be reconciled if we understand it to be describing a variety of entirely different circumstances and intentions.

There are different military benefits to being able to shoot quickly compared to being able to shoot powerfully. Although seasoned with biased and boastful exaggeration, the contrast between strong shooting and quick shooting was recorded in an account of the Persian wars by the Roman writer Procopius in the 6th century AD:

For while their missiles were incomparably more frequent, since the Persians are almost all bowmen and they learn to make their shots much more rapidly than any other men, still the bows which sent the arrows were weak and not very tightly strung, so that their missiles, hitting a corselet, perhaps, or helmet or shield of a Roman warrior, were broken off and had no power to hurt the man who was hit. The Roman bowmen are always slower indeed, but inasmuch as their bows are extremely stiff and very tightly strung, and one might add that they are handled by stronger men, they easily slay much greater numbers of those they hit than do the Persians, for no armour proves an obstacle to the force of their arrows. (Procopius 2007: 169–70)

DRAW-WEIGHTS

It was an aspiration of early Chinese military archers to be able to penetrate seven layers of leather – this was the thickness of a helmet where it was densest, by the ear (Selby 2000: 132) – and shooting powerful bows remained central to Chinese archery culture right up to the end of the Manchu era. As late as 1934 George Cameron Stone, who had been to China some years earlier, observed that 'Bows of 150 pounds are by no means rare in China … The bows that I saw in Peking … were huge, about six feet long strung, with a cross section at the handle of nearly two square inches. They were said to have a pull of about 200 pounds and looked it' (Stone 1961: 134). Not only did the Manchu use the composite bow to a later date than other cultures, they also kept meticulous records, and it is from these that we can glean some insight into the range of draw-weights that were employed; a spectrum that most probably applies equally to the bows of other cultures.

Official documents from 1736, when archery was still a highly valued battlefield skill in China, record detailed test results for the 3,200 men of the elite Hangzhou banner corps. A relatively small group – 80 men – proved their capacity to use bows between 147lb and 173lb. However, the majority – 2,200 men – shot bows in a range between 80lb and 133lb. Lower down the field were 920 bannermen, who were only able to manage bows of 67lb draw-weight or less (Dekker 2012: 103). How much less is not specified, but I would presume there would be nobody shooting less than 60lb. More than two-thirds were in the 80lb to 133lb range. By today's general archery standards these were strong shooters, but there is nothing astonishing about their abilities – many historical archers today shoot bows above 100lb draw-weight and a much larger number can manage bows above 80lb draw-weight. These are not people of superhuman strength; they have simply applied themselves to training in the appropriate techniques for shooting heavy bows, which are quite different from those employed for recreational archery.

The English war-bow archer Joe Gibbs, at full draw with a Crimean Tatar-style bow made by Adam Karpowicz. It has a 180lb draw-weight at 31 inches. Joe is using a Mediterranean three-finger draw because that is what he is familiar with, but he demonstrates even so that men with the right training could shoot bows of such immense power. Joe is of modest stature, though obviously fit and well-muscled. He reports that once the *siyahs* came into play, after about 18 inches, the bow became significantly easier to draw and that there was no stacking. At the time of writing he had only shot it on a couple of occasions, but in a comparison test with an English longbow of identical draw-weight, the Crimean Tatar bow shot further. He used the same arrow (2.1oz with 7-inch fletchings) for both shots. Weather conditions were adverse for achieving a long-distance shot, especially with such a heavy missile, but the arrow from the English longbow made 298 yards, whereas from the composite bow, it reached 320 yards. (Photograph by Kirsty Gibbs)

There was a distinction between the maximum weight a soldier was able to draw, holding it steady without shake, and the weight he was able to shoot with effectively. The data quoted above is derived from shooting tests in which candidates had to drive their arrows into a target. In military examinations all bannermen were additionally required to draw, but not shoot, 160lb as proof of their strength. Gao Ying advised shooting half the poundage an individual could pull. This fits well with the Manchu statistics, showing that most archers could shoot 80lb or more. What the Manchu data reveals more than anything else, however, is that there was a very wide diversity in draw-weight capability, and that even shooting 60lb and over was within an acceptable range.

In 1727 the Chinese emperor railed against a trend among younger men to advance to heavier and heavier draw-weight bows too quickly and to get injured in the process, considering them to be overambitious: 'If there are those who wish to learn how to use a hard bow, they should practice naturally, gradually increasing the strength of the bow ... Besides, using a hard bow on horseback is difficult, so what is the advantage? A bow that is of strength six [80lb] or greater is enough' (quoted in Elliott 2001: 180). Here is an extremely valuable guide as to the sort of draw-weights that we might expect from a horse-archer, and an acknowledgement that it is harder to draw a heavy bow from the saddle than it is on foot. With this in mind, and also taking into account the acceptability, just nine years later, of archers shooting bows in the 60lb bracket, it would be reasonable to deduce that the average horse-archer, across all cultures, probably drew a bow within the 60lb to 80lb range.

The more spectacular draw-weights were reserved for infantry archers. Even among these brawny bowmen, the 80lb to 130lb grade, the main cadre of Hangzhou bannermen, would seem the most plausible

Manchu infantry archers (opposite)

Manchu infantry archers attacking the distinctive tower fortifications of a village during the Jinchuan wars. During the Qing Dynasty (1644–1911) Chinese forces fought two wars against the Jinchuan tribes of Sichuan province, the first in 1747–49 and the second during 1770–76, which led to a final conquest of the region by the Qing. Although the Manchu also used muskets, they continued to rely heavily on the bow even at this late date; it was innate to their military culture. Archery was promoted heavily in the army as an affirmation of Manchurian martial heritage. The rebellious Jinchuan tribes lived in inaccessible, mountainous country. With its stealth and lightweight portability, the bow was ideally suited to these campaigns, which involved sniping, ambush and raid.

Images in art depicting the fighting typically show this type of guerrilla skirmish, with archers shooting on the move or shielded by features in the landscape as they prepare to storm the citadels. Incendiary arrows were especially useful to set conflagrations within the towers and to flush out those taking refuge. Once the Jinchuan were out in the open, fleet-footed in their natural environment, there was an advantage in having fast-moving, hard-hitting bowmen who could hunt them down before they could disappear into the landscape. By comparison, musketeers were too slow.

spectrum. Then, as now, there would have been men of exceptional ability – quite a few of them but exceptional even so – and it was they who drew the most powerful bows: over 130lb on horseback and up to 200lb on foot. These are the men and the bows that achieved the feats of legends, the men who drove arrows deep into wooden blocks and who had the ability to pierce through a shield, a mail coat and an arm, as Anna Komnene described.

ARROWS AND ARMOUR

In addition to the wide-range of draw-weights used, there was wide variation in arrow types and the armours designed to defeat them. Less-well-off troops might have nothing more than a felt or padded coat – good enough against the cudgelling blows of a mace or even a strike from a sword, but only of small benefit against arrows, even those tipped with bone rather than iron. Marauding bands of horse-archers – the Xiongnu, the Avars, the Huns, the Tatars, the Mongols – who, as well as facing armies in the field, terrorized unarmoured villagers in waves of territorial expansion, frequently used arrowheads fashioned from bone. Bodkin-shaped bone arrowheads can be surprisingly effective and I have witnessed them, shot from modest weight bows, punching through a replica plywood shield. However, when the need arose, all these armies also had a variety of highly effective arrowheads forged from iron.

Marco Polo reported that 'Every [Mongol] is ordered to carry into battle sixty arrows, thirty smaller ones for piercing and thirty larger with broad heads for discharging at close quarters' (quoted in Turnbull 2003: 47). Some 60 years earlier, Giovanni da Pian del Carpine – author of the *Ystoria Mongalorum* and papal legate to the Great Khan – observed that 'When they come in sight of the enemy they attack at once, each one shooting three or four arrows at their adversaries' (quoted in Turnbull 2003: 48). This sounds very much like a description of burst-shooting tactics, of galloping in and letting fly as many arrows as possible in the few seconds available at reasonable range (60–20 yards) during a wheeling charge at the enemy's line; perhaps shooting the smaller arrows from further away and saving a broadhead for the moment of greatest proximity. Of course, the optimal arrow for the task depended on an enemy's armour and the composite bow was challenged by many sophisticated armour designs.

A common form of armour in the Ancient World was constructed by overlapping small scales of either hardened leather or metal (bronze or iron). These were stitched onto several layers of linen backing. I had a replica of an Egyptian-style scale armour built, based on an example from the tomb of Tutankhamun. I tested it at ten paces against my 75lb draw-weight angular bow, shooting a bronze arrowhead, mounted on a bamboo shaft, with an acacia foreshaft. It made a perceptible mark, but bounced off with no hint of penetration. Lightweight armour of this sort was equally suitable for the protection of chariot horses, but it would probably have been no match for the Pharaoh Amenhotep II and his mighty bow who, from his chariot, shot at copper targets one palm – around 4 inches –

Replica of Egyptian scale armour made by Todd Feinman. This was constructed from rawhide scales, coloured with milk paint and sealed with shellac. The scales have been sewn with cord to six layers of gathered linen. A further 12 layers of linen were stitched together to form the type of under-armour backing that was likely to have been worn. Each scale overlaps not only vertically but also horizontally, so that at any point an arrow hits, it is obstructed by three layers. Moreover, the nature of the scale assembly over a multilayered fabric backing produces a repelling spring-like effect on contact. (KH)

thick. His chronicler reported that 'It was really a
deed which had never been done nor heard of
by report: shooting at a target of copper an
arrow which came out and dropped to
the ground' (quoted in Pritchard 1969:
244). Allowing for a certain amount
of pandering to Pharaonic vanity, such
stories are a useful benchmark for defining
what was extraordinary and unusual. It may be
that such a feat was possible, but the point about it
is that it was exceptional; not normal. Of greater interest
to the student of the bow is what was commonplace and that, I would
suggest, is that armour worked reasonably well against archery – though
not infallibly, of course.

Armour of great ingenuity was developed to keep its wearer as safe as
possible. A medieval Persian set of instructions for making a leather *josan/
jawshan* – a body armour of rectangular plates laced together – details
depilating camel hides in a solution of milk and soda and then cutting
the leather into the appropriately shaped plates. When dry, four layers
of a special glue compound were applied to the surface of each plate,
allowing drying-time between each coat. This 'glue' included granules of
red copper and crushed corundite (emery), as well as two other substances
that have not yet been identified by translators (Nicolle 2002: 179). It
seems reasonable to assume that the unidentified ingredients provided the
adhesive solution to bind the materials and apply the coating. Furthermore,
it seems probable that such composite layering of leather, metal and rock
would create shock-absorbing and surface-hardened armour, capable of
repelling arrows from all but the strongest bows.

Few armours gave protection against arrows to the same extent as
a *kazaghand*, a multilayered armoured coat that was worn throughout
the Near East and Persia by those who could afford it, and also adopted
by some European crusaders. In a slide of pronunciation, the *kazaghand*
became known as the *jazerant* as it emigrated to the backs of crusading
knights. If the men that Ibn Shaddād witnessed with arrows sticking in
them after the battle of Arsuf were in fact dismounted knights wearing
the *jazerant*, the story becomes more credible without downplaying the
considerable power of the Saracens' bows.

This is especially so if we consider that the 'porcupining' of these poor
fellows was most probably inflicted by horse-archers, men who were
shooting bows that were perhaps in the 60lb to 80lb range. Moreover,
their deployment had been directed to disrupt and annoy, a tactic requiring
fistfuls of slender, lightweight arrows that could be loosed with repetitive
bursts of speed-shooting. There should be no surprise if a combination
of relatively light bows and arrows against a supreme model of armour
resulted in superficial damage and few fatalities. Even so, it would not
follow that the archery had not achieved its intended goal – if that goal
was to harass. As I noted in *The Longbow* (Loades 2013: 72), modern
analysts tend to be preoccupied with penetration, considering it the sole
gauge of an archer's effectiveness. It is a false measure.

TACTICAL IMPACT

The effectiveness of military archery has to be assessed according to its intended purpose: whether it is to kill or wound enemy combatants with powerful shots that either penetrate or cause catastrophic blunt-trauma in a battle of attrition, or whether it is to harass, unnerve, control and contain the movements of enemy forces with incessant showers of arrows. Wallop and saturation require different approaches with both tactics and equipment. Each should be weighed on a separate scale.

There is a correlation between the power of a bow and the ability to shoot it rapidly. Moreover, the selection of arrow type was informed, not only by the armour of an opponent but also by the style of shooting – rapid burst-shooting tactics required slimmer, lighter arrows, not only for their ease in management but also because an archer could carry them in greater numbers. Snipers and those in siege situations were advantaged when shooting especially powerful bows with thumping, heavy arrows. Infantry archers shooting en masse at range required heavy bows in order to make the distance. (See my observations on the military expedients of long-range shooting and husbanding arrow stocks in Loades 2013: 65–70.) They equally had use for heavy bows when shooting at relatively close targets, when the intention was to make every arrow count with a knockout punch – this was the military thinking of the Manchu. Rate of shooting was of lesser importance in these instances because the archers were either in a defended position, behind walls or pavises, or because the sheer numbers of a large archer contingent generated a sufficiently impressive volume of shafts. However, infantry archers deployed as skirmishers, shooting rapidly and on the move, were better served with slightly lighter bows and lighter arrows.

Similarly, horse-archers shot lighter bows – compared to those of strongbow infantry. All bows had to be of a useful military weight, of course, but as we have seen this covered a very wide range. A horse-archer can ride reasonably close to his target and so can to a large extent compensate for lower poundage – a 70lb or 80lb bow could still deliver an arrow with an impressive whack at 20, 30 or 40 yards. Persistent harassment by horse-archers, the psychological equivalent to a constant artillery barrage, ground away at an enemy's resolve and put him on edge. It wearied him. Not every arrow had to kill; it simply had to be a threat and an irritant, and to pack a sufficient degree of painful punch. Moreover, such assaults could be executed with relatively little risk to the attacking force, and they could be sustained for days.

Whether or not there was a heavy casualty rate, one of the most effective aspects of military archery was that it could enable one army to keep opposing regiments pinned in position: it offered control of the battlefield. This was particularly so with the use of horse-archers. A common tactic during the Crusades, as well as other conflicts, was to shoot at the horses. Armour for horses was available with varying degrees of completeness, but horses nevertheless remained larger and more vulnerable targets than their well-armoured riders. Moreover, even seasoned warhorses could be distressed and panicked by the sting and terror of an arrowstorm. Anna Komnene recalls an incident, when a troop of horse-archers were sent against the Norman military leader Bohemond's cavalry: 'they rained down arrows on their mounts and thus created a scene of chaos for the riders' (Komnene 2009: 143). The tactic was used here in the context of pursuit – to keep driving an enemy off without engaging him in direct contact. Horse-archers, and other light cavalry, were also of considerable value in the rout, in sealing a victory.

In *Taktika*, a book of military tactics written by the Byzantine Emperor Leo VI (r. 886–912), he advised his archers to shoot at the horses of the Arabs because it would put them to flight: 'They will do this for two reasons, namely because of their desire to save their horses, which are highly prized, and not easily procured, and because they want to save themselves as well through saving the horses' (quoted in Dennis 2010: 129). Even so, a successor emperor – Nikephoros II Phokas (963–69) – cautioned that if Arab horsemen were driven off, it would be a mistake to pursue them; they were somewhat fleeter than Bohemond's cavalry: 'When pursued they are not overtaken and, aided by the speed of their horses, they quickly counter-attack and strike against our men. It does no good at all to go chasing after them' (quoted in Dennis 1985: 104).

The effectiveness of the horse-archer was inextricably connected not only to the power of his bow but also to the celerity and stamina of his horse. In pitched battle, horse-archers were used very effectively both for encirclement, flanking manoeuvres, what the Mongols termed the *tulughma*, and for a constant stream of attacks. When the Magyars and the Patzinaks raised their challenge to the Byzantine Empire, the Arab historian al-Mas'ūdī gave a detailed account of their tactics during a campaign in 934:

> The engagement began with the horsemen of the right wing attacking the main battle of the Byzantines, showering it with arrows, and taking up a new position on the left. Then they of the left wing likewise advanced and shot against the Byzantine main battle, changing over to the right side of the line. So the mounted bands kept wheeling across the Byzantine front, grinding away at it like millstones. (Quoted in Jankovich 1971: 103)

This fluidity characterized a fundamental difference in military thinking between East and West; between fighting from entrenched, defended positions and the mobility of the horse-archer. Even when mounted, European knights formed moving walls, as fixed in formation as any fortress, relying on impact for effect. They had to make contact to engage an enemy. However, the horse-archer was able to strike at distance, always able to elude direct contact unless it was on his own terms; unless he had softened an enemy sufficiently. Moreover, he was able to remain continuously mobile, forever changing the direction and timing of his attack on both the battlefield and the march. It gave him a versatility and adaptability unmatched by any other type of combatant.

There can be no doubt that the composite bow, in its myriad manifestations, has also been a highly effective weapon for the infantry archer – both on the battlefield and in siege warfare. It was in the hands of the horse-archer, however, that it has had its most lasting impact.

Developed primarily to withstand arrow strikes, the *jazerant* was a complex, layered defence; this replica section was made by Deborah Lee. A single garment, it was worn over a shirt and from the inside out consisted of: a rabbit skin *gambeson*, made of stitched-together, hair-on rabbit pelts (rabbit is an especially dense but lightweight pelt) sandwiched between layers of thick linen; a full-length coat of riveted mail covering the arms and extending to below the knees; a second, outer *gambeson* that was tightly stuffed with silk waste; a half-length coat of riveted mail; and an outer covering of brocade silk. The entire armour was riveted through with pigtail rivets, which gathered together all the layers into quilted pockets. This quilting effect made all the materials – pelt, linens, mail, stuffing – considerably denser and less penetrable. There would also have been another layer of linen on the inside to cover the coils of the pigtail rivets. *Jazerants* opened at the front, so that they could be donned quickly, in the manner of an overcoat. The skirts were divided front and back, so that the horseman could wear it in the saddle. (Photographs courtesy of Nicholas Checksfield)

CONCLUSION

The study of the composite bow, once solely the preserve of a few gentlemen antiquarians, is now enjoying considerable popularity. This coincides with a deepening interest in traditional and historical archery in general. A growing band of skilled artisans are practising the arts of the composite bowyer. Replica bows, built from genuine horn and sinew, are available to purchase more than ever before. Some archers are conditioning themselves to shoot bows of historical poundage, and shooting with a thumb-ring has become an increasingly familiar sight at archery ranges. All this sets the stage for much-needed empirical experimentation to understand more about how these bows were used and what they were capable of achieving. There are now many useful independent websites, but the Asian Traditional Archery Research Network (ATARN) is the central body through which all meaningful online research is disseminated.

Strongly linked to the resurgence of interest in making and shooting the composite bow is the growth in popularity of horse-archery, both as a competitive sport and as a pure martial art. In some countries, namely those having a strong horse-archer heritage, it has become a statement of cultural identity, with practitioners often dressing in traditional garb and using only the bow of that culture. In places without a national tradition, horse-archers shoot an assortment of bow forms, including modern hybrid styles, and in a variety of attire. Archery with the composite bow is a living art and the best are beginning to shoot with the power, the speed and the accuracy of horse-archers from the past.

Today's horse-archers develop a connection to their horse, to their bow and to themselves that a warrior from the steppes would have understood and that a noble *fāris* would have admired. Study of the composite bow is a gateway to learning about a diverse gamut of peoples and historical periods; a study of infinite fascination and reward. When so much historical study is nationalistic in character, this extraordinary, beautiful weapon opens new horizons for cross-cultural knowledge and discovery.

BIBLIOGRAPHY

CSPF = 'Elizabeth: July 1582, 21–25', in Calendar of State Papers Foreign, Elizabeth, Vol. 16, May–December 1582, ed. Arthur John Butler: 170–88. http://www.british-history.ac.uk/cal-state-papers/foreign/vol16/pp170-188 (accessed 2 May 2015).

Dekker, Peter (2012). 'A Practical Guide to Manchu Military Archery', in *Journal of Chinese Martial Studies*, 2012, Issue 6: 80–173.

Dennis, George, trans. & ed. (1985). *Three Byzantine Military Treatises*. Cambridge, MA: Harvard UP.

Dennis, George, trans. & ed. (2010). *The Taktika of Leo VI*. Cambridge, MA: Harvard UP.

Elliott, Mark (2001). *The Manchu Way*. Redwood City, CA: Stanford UP.

Faris, N.A. & Elmer, R.P. (1945). *Arab Archery*. Princeton, NJ: Princeton UP.

Heath, E.G. (1971). *The Grey Goose Wing*. London: Osprey Publishing.

Herodotus, trans. A.D. Godley (2013). *Complete Works*. Hastings: Delphi Classics.

Jankovich, Miklos (1971). *They Rode Into Europe*. London: Harrap.

Khorasani, Dr Manouchehr Moshtagh (2013). *Persian Archery and Swordsmanship*. Frankfurt-am-Main: Niloufar Books.

Klopsteg, Paul (1987). *Turkish Archery and the Composite Bow*. Manchester: Simon Archery Foundation, The Manchester Museum.

Komnene, Anna, trans. E.R.A. Sewter (2009). *The Alexiad*. Harmondsworth: Penguin.

Koppedrayer, Kay (2002). *Kay's Thumbring Book*. Ontario: Blue Vase Press.

Latham, J. D. & Paterson, W.F. (1970). *Saracen Archery*. London: The Holland Press.

Liao Wanzhen, trans. Stephen Selby (1999). 'Whistling arrows and arrows whistles'. Asian Traditional Archery Research Network. http://www.atarn.org/chinese/whistle/whistle.htm (accessed 12 September 2015).

Loades, Mike (2013). *The Longbow*. Oxford: Osprey Publishing.

Marcellinius, Ammianus, trans. W. Hamilton (1986). *The Later Roman Empire*. Harmondsworth: Penguin.

Nicolle, David (1994). *Saracen Faris*. London: Osprey Publishing.

Nicolle, David (2001). 'A Mamluk Training Manual', in *Osprey Military Journal*, 2001, Issue 3/5: 42–49.

Nicolle, David (2002). *A Companion to Medieval Arms and Armour*. Woodbridge: The Boydell Press.

Öztopçu, Kurtuluş, trans. (1986). *A 14th Century Mamluk-Kipchak Military Treatise: Münyetü'l-Ġuzāt*. http://www.scribd.com/doc/114356754/Munyatu-l-Guzat#scribd (accessed 21 August 2015).

Paterson, W.F. (1984). *Encyclopaedia of Archery*. London: Robert Hale Ltd.

Pritchard, J.B. (1969). *Ancient Near Eastern Texts Relating to the Old Testament*. Princeton, NJ: Princeton UP.

Pritchard, J.B. (2011). *The Ancient Near East – An Anthology of Texts and Pictures*. Princeton, NJ: Princeton UP.

Procopius, trans. H.B. Dewing (2007). *History of the Wars: The Persian War*. New York, NY: Cosimo.

Ray, Purnima, trans. (2014). *Vasistha's Dhanurveda Samhita*. Yokohama: JP Publishing House.

Selby, Stephen (2000). *Chinese Archery*. Hong Kong: Hong Kong University Press.

Selby, Stephen & Karpowicz, Adam (2010). 'Scythian Bow from Xinjang', in *Journal of the Society of Archer Antiquaries*, Vol. 53: 94–102.

Smail, R.C. (1995). *Crusading Warfare 1097–1193*. Cambridge: Cambridge University Press.

Stone, George Cameron (1961). *A Glossary of the Construction, Decoration, and Use of Arms and Armor in All Countries and in All Times*. New York, NY: Jack Brussel. Reprint of 1934 edition.

Tian, Jie & Ma, Justin (2015). *The Way of Archery: A 1637 Chinese Military Training Manual*. Atglen, PA: Schiffer Publishing.

Thompson, Maurice (1878). *The Witchery of Archery*. New York, NY: Charles Scribner's Sons.

Turnbull, Stephen (2003). *Mongol Warrior 1200–1350*. Oxford: Osprey Publishing.

Verbruggen, J.F. (1997). *The Art of Warfare in Western Europe during the Middle Ages*. Woodbridge: The Boydell Press.

INDEX